Ride on the Wing of the Eagle

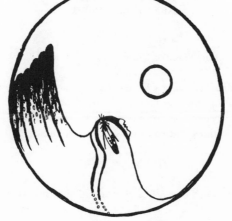

... Viewing life from a higher perspective

Sheila Griffin

MYSTIC MOON PUBLISHING

Ride on the Wing of the Eagle
Published by Mystic Moon Publishing
Santa Fe, New Mexico
1-800-301-5107

Copyright © 1998 Sheila Griffin
ISBN 0-9659346-8-3

First Edition 1998

Library of Congress Cataloging-in-Publication Data

Griffin, Sheila, 1944–
Ride on the wing of the eagle :
viewing life from a higher perspective / by Sheila Griffin.
p.   cm.
ISBN 0-9659346-8-3 (alk. paper)
1. Spiritual life.
2. Shamanism—Miscellanea.
3. Indians of North America—Colorado—Religion—Miscellanea.
I. Title.
BL624.G739   1997
299' .7—dc21
97-27353
CIP

Text illustrations by Pbaquenee, Spruce Standing Deer
and Sheila Griffin

TO MY CHILDREN,

MY GRANDCHILDREN

AND FUTURE GENERATIONS

TABLE OF CONTENTS

Introduction   9

CHAPTER ONE: Beginning the Journey   15

CHAPTER TWO: Acknowledging Fear   31

CHAPTER THREE: Reality Fear and Illusory Fear   45

CHAPTER FOUR: Fear of Death   57

CHAPTER FIVE: Vaulting the Barriers of Separation
    and Alienation   69

CHAPTER SIX: Nurturing Through Nature   83

CHAPTER SEVEN: Accessing Personal Power   93

CHAPTER EIGHT: Meditation   105

CHAPTER NINE: The Shield of Letting Go   119

CHAPTER TEN: Going Beyond Fear   135

CHAPTER ELEVEN: Outrageousness   145

CHAPTER TWELVE: The Shield of Power   163

CHAPTER THIRTEEN: Ride on the Wing of the Eagle   175

Appendix   181

Afterword   185

About the Author   187

My thanks to the earth
and all her treasures,
the creepy crawlers,
the rock people,
the winged ones,
the standing people,
the four legged,
and the two legged.

MITAKUYE OYASIN
(LAKOTA FOR "ALL MY RELATIONS")

Walk beside me on the "red road."

We will stumble along the way.

We will feel fear.

We will feel it in our emotions, our body,
   our humanness.

We will cry out.

We will walk on.

We will experience fear and feel it transform.

We will ride on the wing of the eagle.

INTRODUCTION

F ear is pervasive in our world, and I have experienced, like many others, my own personal fears. This book integrates stories of my journey on the "Red Road" over the last several years that have connected me to my own Blackfoot roots and continues to play an important role in my life today.

I have used concepts and spiritual beliefs from Native American traditions and Buddhist teachings. The most profound influence to my role as a psychotherapist has been the Buddhist concept of mindfulness. It has helped me to be more aware of what is taking place around me and within me. It has given me a sense of relaxation that I do not have to always *do* something or *fix* a problem that one might be experiencing. I can just "be" when it is appropriate not to act, and when action is needed, act with more clarity.

As a person on my life journey, being mindful has helped me to notice what is in my world and then decide how I want to interact.

Native American spirituality has enabled me to be in my world in a special way, noticing the unique gifts that nature has bestowed upon me. Bringing my awareness into nature has allowed me to become a part of nature and to learn from her.

Working through fear has been a transformational process for me, and I hope what I have to share will also contribute to your journey.

For many years I have worked with people to help them discover their own inner knowing. Using hypnosis in the process has facilitated this inner search more expediently than any other modality that I have practiced. It has been my intention during my years as a therapist to give people the opportunity to become their own healers. Everyone has that capacity, and because you are reading this book now, you are ready to discover this creative healing potential within.

As a hypnotherapist, I have had the privilege of witnessing this healing journey for many of my clients. I have seen astounding results relating to low self-esteem, communication difficulties, phobias, depression, relationships, addictions and sexual abuse. People who have been in traditional therapy are often looking for something more, usually a connection with their higher Self, and this book is an attempt to support you in this inner search.

This book, however, is not about hypnotherapy. It is mentioned here only to help you understand how you can work with the unconscious mind which is the gateway to the higher Self. It is about our connection to the earth, to each other and to our higher Self. As we become closer to nature, we can begin to see that we are a part of that creation, and integration of the gifts of our environment help us to live more comfortably in it. If we are receptive, we will find many of the answers to life's questions in nature. Throughout the text, I emphasize how important it is to respect and honor the things in nature. There is a lot of wisdom to be found in the gifts of the earth. When we become aware of our environment in nature, we become more aware in our personal lives and interactions with others. As we begin to experience our relationship with people in a more diverse way, we can connect with each other as extensions of ourselves.

Although there is only one chapter on the Shield of Letting Go this book is also about letting go—letting go every moment just as we exhale every breathe we take. It is about letting go of our past whether it be the moment, the hour, the day, or years that have come before. We learn from the past, but holding on to it does not allow us to be in the present. Being in the moment helps us to connect with our higher Self.

There is nothing that our higher Self does not know, yet we seem to be cut off from that sacred part of ourselves. The guidance we get from Great Spirit and our spirit helpers supports us in tapping into our higher Self as well.

Each of the personal experiences in this book is followed by an exercise or visualization that you might find helpful. (See the Appendix to assist you in beginning this process.) I have found them useful both personally and in my private practice as a therapist. When reading the stories and working with the exercises, it is especially helpful to apply them to your own experience. Every person is, of course, different, and each individual experience of self, others and his or her environment needs to be worked with specifically. You may relate to some of the stories and not others. Take what you find valuable for yourself. The process involves trusting and loving yourself and knowing that you possess the power that you need to be all that you desire in this life. Oftentimes, I encounter clients who have continually sought the help of a psychic. They are always looking for answers outside of themselves. Although many psychics are legitimate and apt at tapping into the universal consciousness, frequenting them does not allow you to develop and draw from your higher Self. This is where your power lies! We spend too much time depending on others to tell us what to do or to "fix it" for us. Lets not continue feeding our dependency—we have a wealth of material within us in which to draw.

Each of us is a powerhouse of knowledge, of universal energy. The information contained here is an offering to you to believe in yourself and to allow transformation to take place in your life.

CHAPTER ONE

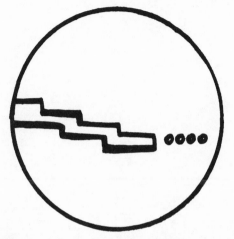

Beginning the Journey

Look to our individual journey and the role
we each play in the collective.
Only through this relationship
can positive change begin.

I began my journey to Shamanism without even knowing I was on the road. I began when I moved to Boulder, Colorado, from Dallas, Texas, several years ago with my husband, Tom. The long, arduous trip by car was rewarded as we entered the enchantment of New Mexico. The sun was taking its nightly dive to the other side of the world and left us with a palette of blue, orange and pink splashed across the horizon. I had much anticipation coming to this part of the country, and although I had never been to Colorado, there was a longing within me to be there.

As we drove Highway 36 from Denver, the mountains to the west grew in their massiveness, towering like great earth gods above Boulder which is nestled lovingly at their base. Scattered at the base of the foothills, the lights of the small city appeared like the night lights of many tiny children bedded down to sleep. I soon set up a psychotherapy practice in this cradle town and began my work on a master's degree at The Naropa Institute. It was no surprise that I was drawn to Colorado— the energy affords healing on many levels, and that is what my body, mind and spirit had been seeking. I have since come to understand that Boulder is a place that precipitates working on your issues whether you like it or not; therefore, it can be a challenge living in the energy there.

Entering Boulder was for me like being born into a new world. Unlike my entrance into the world as an infant, my entrance into this new experience was supportive. As a newborn infant I had collided with an environment that did not support my right to be safe in my world. The environment did not contain quite enough nurturing for me to feel that I could fully express myself in it without internalizing fear.

When the time came for me to interact more with my environment outside of the home, I had a harder time feeling safe. As the years passed, my fear was constantly reinforced by the news media. Learning that my world was not a safe place, I rarely took risks. Instead, I played it safe. And so it went. When I had children of my own I wished that my house was made of glass so I could watch over them when they were out playing.

Entering this new energetic field in Boulder gave me the opportunity to go into the fear and work with it. The opportunity to do this came when I least expected it.

There have been books written where seekers of wisdom and self knowledge were shown in a vision or dream who their teacher would be, and they would travel many miles to be with this teacher and upon their arrival would be greeted with the words, "I have been waiting for you." Others have been going about their ordinary lives and the teacher showed up at their front door. You do not have to go to a distant land or hope that one day your teacher will just show up. Instead, there are other ways.

After settling in Boulder, I met a Native American woman who became a catalyst for me to explore new ways of using my own gifts of intuition and power. I did not seek her nor did she show up mysteriously. I met her through a friend for the purpose of having her facilitate a sweat lodge ceremony for a workshop that I was facilitating for a group of women. I had found out years earlier that my great grandmother was half Blackfoot, so I wanted to learn more about my Native American heritage and spirituality. After talking it over, we decided to do some personal work together. Her name is Raven. Our meeting would be the beginning of a relationship that would bring love, joy, excitement, adventure and also put me right up against the fear that lay dormant inside, yet seeped out to influence and restrict my life.

Raven and I made a commitment to walk the Red Road through a formal ceremony with the pipe called an Opahe Ceremony. We made our commitment in a small, cluttered room in Raven's house that doubled as a living room and a ceremonial space. Draped from the walls were what appeared to be shields, some with skins of animals, some painted in a curious fashion. I wondered what meaning they held. One shield had the skin of a coyote stretched over a hoop made from a willow branch. The coyote head was in tact with the skin and fur tightly pulled over bone. The hollows where the eyes were looked blank and dark. Strips of brightly colored red cloth hung down from the bottom rim almost touching the floor. Another shield had rawhide stretched around the circumference, and in the center a painted eagle flew.

As I stood surveying the room, Raven came out of the kitchen with a smile, little wrinkles branching out from the corners of her dark eyes. She exemplified the image of femininity with her curved body and ample hips. Her bluish-black hair hung loosely down her back, streaks of white running through it from her temples. She was not wearing makeup and her face looked strong and her eyes piercing, yet there was a softness about her. Her full body moved in a undulating way, swaying from side to side as she walked. The feeling of love and acceptance radiated from her.

I agreed to walk the Red Road (Native American way) as Raven would instruct me to, meeting with her every couple of weeks for our work together. Working with an urban shaman was not what I had expected, but it turned out to be the perfect situation for us both, and we were able to get a lot accomplished during our time together.

Raven guided me to situations that caused events
and learning experiences to naturally unfold so
that the earth and her creatures were the real
teachers.

Discernment is important in choosing to work
with someone outside of yourself. Remember that
no one is greater and more knowledgeable than
you when it comes to walking your path. At one
point during my journey I became confused. I
took a class through the Naropa Institute at the
same time I was working with Raven. I heard
things in class that contradicted some of Raven's
teachings. One day I cried all the way home from
class and then realized that I needed to look at my
own truth in any given situation. From there forward I would always check in to "feel" if what was
being given or taught to me was in alignment with
my own "feeling" of what is true for me. When we
put our trust in others to know our truth instead
of finding our own inner knowing, we are giving
our personal power away. When you are working
with someone on your journey, you are entitled to

know what their intentions are in any given moment, how and why they want you to do something and that all your questions will be answered and explained. It is important that your teacher or helper empowers you to seek your own truth—no one else can do it for you. Raven was such a teacher.

Raven gave me a talking staff made from petrified wood. She found it while walking on the beach in California several years before and had kept it among her treasures until the right time came to make it come alive. She painted it with a gold beak, gold spots and adorned it with wild turkey feathers and the down of an owl. The head of the staff looked like an eagle's head. My staff would be held by many hands and hold secrets, feelings and prayers. I use this staff in groups that I facilitate, and it has helped each person holding it to speak from their heart and be heard by others in the group as well. Hopefully it helped to facilitate the journey of all who held it.

My journey was one of Kimimila (Lakota for

"transformation") through fear. My main focus is the Native American teachings I have experienced, specifically connecting to Mother Earth, interlaced with the concept of mindfulness meditation from Buddhist teachings. You are invited to relive this journey with me through these pages. As we move out of our past, live in the moment and experience ourselves, others and the planet as one, there is really nothing to fear. The struggle is an inner one, and it is there that peace needs to begin.

Fear is a common thread that binds us—with each other, with our society and with ourselves. As a dichotomy, it also separates us. It is an emotion, an energy that keeps us stuck in unhealthy relation- ships, unfulfilling jobs and most of all, in experi- encing life to the fullest. I have often experienced fear. I cannot define it precisely, and I cannot tell you specifically where it came from, but it has been there. I have helped my clients overcome their spe- cific fears so that they can function in their lives. I function in mine. The difference was to "let go" at a deeper level that permeated my entire soul. At that level everything else automatically eased up. My body became more relaxed. My mind became more of a friend instead of resistant baggage to be hauled around with a never ending file of negative phrases that were recklessly flung about—keeping me from being powerful, relaxed and joyful in my life. This is what I wanted. This is why I chose to walk the Red Road through my fear.

The extent to which we internalize fear is shaped by conditions at birth or before and continues within our family environment. As a child I was afraid of the dark and had nightmares for years. When I had a night fright and went to my mother for comfort she would tell me to build a house in my mind and furnish each room until I fell asleep. My mother was not a physical nurturer, instead she nurtured us with good cooking and a spotless home. She did her best and was parenting from her learned experiences. A hug and a "I love you" would have served me better.

This lack of support came not only from within my family structure but also from my cultural structure. Like many others, I learned how to be fearful from my experiences, from watching others and from our cultural dynamics.

When I became a little older, it was a family privilege to stay up and watch television, and the nightly news became a ritual—then I got to see how people all over the world hurt and kill each other. It would be naive to think that we need to be taught that we live in Utopia, but at the same time do we need to be over stimulated with negative information? It is no wonder I later began a nightly ritual of double checking to see that my doors were locked at night. I was keeping a hall light burning for the next generation of fearful children until I decided to change my relationship with fear.

I was also born into an existing world. Familial/cultural dynamics did not begin when I arrived; I was deposited right in the middle of them. I was constantly trying to fit into an environment that already existed, and it was a difficult thing to do. In attempting to conform to the shifts of the cultural drama, I created my own personal drama around that dynamic.

What can we do about the fear that permeates our society and the world over? To make a difference in our culture and on the planet we need to work on having a "love" consciousness. We can each do this by expanding our own awareness and by relating to our children and grandchildren and the world with love instead of fear. Some Native Americans consider the generations to come before they do anything that might spoil the earth or their natural heritage. Their history is one of honor and respect for the earth and all her creatures. Why can we not have this same attitude toward a better world consciousness for those who will come after us?

We need to overcome our fears in order to influence positive change in our world so that the generations after us can be born into a more supportive, loving environment. Beginning a personal journey through fear involves commitment. It is taking a stand and saying "I intend to change what is not working for me in my life." The desire to change can be a very powerful motivation to take control of your life. Change can be scary at first. After all, we are used to the way things are, and misery becomes comfortable. If we change so will our world. In order to actualize the joy of living, we need to go beyond our history.

Visualization: *Beginning Your Journey*

Acknowledge where you are now on your path. Assess what you want to change. Ask yourself what is holding you back from expressing yourself fully in the world. You may already know and have been too fearful or doubtful to move ahead. If you are confused, set your intention and wait for your answer. If you already know, now may be the time to begin your journey of moving through the limitation you have placed on yourself. Start by letting go of past situations and relationships that have kept you stuck so that you can move forward in your life. The following exercise may assist you in this process.

Close your eyes and imagine a person and/or situation from your past that you want to let go of. See this person and/or situation in front of you now. Express what you need to say and how you are feeling in order for your communication to be complete with this person: anger, sadness, etc. Take a deep breath and surround yourself with white light. Listen to hear a message about what you have learned in this past experience with this person. If you are ready to forgive this person, do so.

Now, imagine a cord of light energy connecting you and this person and reach out and sever the cord. See the person moving away from you and feel yourself without the influence of his or her energy. Release that person with love. Take another deep breath and sense your energy field. Is there a feeling of letting go of the person and/or situation? If not, you can repeat this exercise again.

You might also look at how you, as an individual, can influence positive change in the collective environment. As change happens within so will it happen in the world.

CHAPTER TWO

Acknowledging Fear –
Waking Up The Numbness

Open to the fear.
Only when you look into its true nature
will you be able to ride through it.

I traveled from Boulder to the Pine Ridge reservation in South Dakota during the summer of 1992. Raven had suggested that I visit the reservation to see firsthand how her native people lived. As I drove onto the reservation, it was nothing like I had imagined. The land spread out like a green blanket, and the horizon stretched out to meet it. The sky was so expansive that it felt as if I were on top of the world. The clouds hung low in the sky like a soft down comforter inviting my touch. There were miles of rolling hills where the road became a snake winding its way to an unknown destination. With each rise and fall in the road, I was swallowed up by the landscape just ahead. Occasionally, I would see a house trailer positioned like a toy in the distance or a field where horses, wild as the wind, roamed together. There were miles of uninhabited acres with no trees to stop the land from rambling on to what seemed like the edge of the earth.

I made my way to Wounded Knee where I had heard from a friend that several Sundances (ceremony to give honor to Great Spirit or God) would be held. I pulled my Honda up to the dry, dusty parking lot in front of the local grocery store. It was a hot, lazy day and the store had no air conditioner—just a screen door to keep flies out and let in any air that might want to offer some relief. A few locals were standing around inside talking, cold drinks in their hands. I asked if they knew of a Sundance in the area, one that a non-Indian could attend. The shorter of the two Native American men standing by the checkout counter gave me directions, and after buying a soda, I headed for the car. The afternoon sun was high on its path, and the air was clean and smelled of burnt sage as I parked the car in a field where other, older cars and pickup trucks were seated and walked to where the festivities were taking place.

I was the only white person present, and I felt very honored to be accepted there, and at the same time, careful not to offend these Native American people. I sat under an arbor made from the trunks and branches of indigenous trees, which shaded the spectators from the heat of the pulsating sun.

There were many women and children, some sitting leisurely in the shade under the arbor, others standing and dancing in place along with the Sundancers to the drumming and chanting sounds vibrating from the singers and drummers on the other side of the arbor.

Small children were running in and out and around the encampment, barefooted and wearing loose, unpretentious clothes and big smiles. Some of the women were chatting and holding on to children too small to be left unattended. I sat down on the cool grass watching quietly as the Sundancers hung from ropes that were attached to a center tree and pierced to their skin, one rope on each side of their chests. As the Sundancers broke away from the tree, they would dance around the circle; some blowing on eagle bone whistles, bodies glistening with perspiration from the warmth of the summer sun, drops of blood trickling from the wounds on their chests. Giving their blood in this way was their sacrifice to Great Spirit. Sometimes it would take hours for the dancers to break free, and they endured this without food or water. As the day progressed, I noticed that one dancer did have this dilemma. He finally sat down on the ground with his head in his hands, apparently exhausted and disappointed. Several of the other dancers went over to him giving encouragement. He never gave up, and when he broke free from the ropes, I felt the same relief as the others must have felt. As the sundancer joined the other dancers around the ceremonial space, I gazed up at the center tree.

At the top of the tree were banners of various bright colors blowing in the breeze with prayer ties (small pieces of cloth wrapped around tobacco, each made with a prayer) tied at the ends. The tree was a cottonwood and had been chosen from the woods nearby and blessed by the medicine man. It was then carried to the center of the ceremonial space, women holding up the branches while men carried the trunk. The dancers wore brightly colored skirts or dresses and were adorned at the ankles, wrists and crown with wreaths of fresh sage.

At one point during the ceremony, the pipe was offered by the dancers to women standing outside of the circle. These women were evidently chosen for this honor and stood opposite the dancers as a pipe ritual of offering commenced. The women, in turn, passed the pipe to the spectators to smoke. A small, dark woman came to me and held out the pipe. She did not speak to me but motioned for me to smoke. I held the pipe in my hands, reflecting on my first experience with it.

I first began to know the pipe on a day that found the earth covered with the whitest of snow and the brightest of suns overhead. I have always held the pipe in a very timid way, afraid of it in a sense—its power, its mystery. Who am I to hold this pipe? It was the same old story for me—what I am afraid of, I cannot be close to. So it was, the opportunity once again to move through my fear so that I could be close, make the connection and though this pipe feel the love of Great Spirit.

I sat with Raven at the altar in her home. A grey wool blanket with orange, red and yellow woven yarn at each end held ceremonial objects: a statue of a nude woman, an Abalone shell, bowls of sage and cedar, prayer flags and several oil candles. The room was dim and became a little more revealing as Raven lit a candle that was already in its place on the altar between us.

"I have felt for a while now that it is time for

you to become more familiar with the pipe," she said as I sat crossed legged and rigid by her side. Raven's dark eyes glistened in the soft glow of candlelight, fine lines stemming out from the corners like lacy spider webs. I relaxed more and felt my body settle languidly in place beside her.

Raven took me through the steps of filling the pipe with tobacco and lavender. First, I took small pinches between my fingers and offered each pinch to the seven directions starting in the West, then the North, East, South, Above, Below and Center. We sang the pipe song.

When the pipe had been filled, Raven smoked to each of the directions and then handed the pipe to me. Holding the bowl of the pipe to my heart center and the stem to my forehead, I prayed to Great Spirit.

"Great Spirit, I seem always to ask for so many things. Today, I ask for only one thing. Help me to overcome the fear and limitations that have kept me from fully walking this path of life so that I may be of service to others in this world. Help me to not be afraid and to do what it takes to make this happen in a good way."

I felt a connection with the pipe for the first

time as my heart center began to open. It was a feeling that cannot be explained but only experienced. Tears welled up in my eyes and flowed like rivers down my cheeks. The pipe was truly alive! I could feel throughout my being the love and support of Great Spirit.

Following Raven's lead, I then smoked to the seven directions. I felt a little awkward in the mechanics of it all and had to relight the pipe several times, but I knew that the moment was very special for me and that it was a new beginning and a new relationship with the sacred pipe; one that would become my comfort and support.

Bringing my awareness back to the moment, reawakening to the activity of the Sundance, I put the pipe to my lips and smoked. I sat for another hour watching the ceremony conclude.

The afternoon sun was fading, and I was getting tired and hungry. I asked one of the women sitting near me in the arbor if she knew of a place to camp nearby. She motioned for me to wait and ran off. A few minutes later she came bouncing back with another woman who looked like someone of authority. She was the medicine man's wife and greeted me with openness and acceptance.

"I will talk with the medicine man and see if you can camp here," she said. "You can also eat with us as we will be preparing a feast tonight." I felt enamored by her grace and, at the same time, a little apprehensive to stay among their people overnight. A part of me was living in the past—I was fearful of being different and not "fitting in." The people were friendly and did not seem to judge me by the color of my skin. They danced and drummed late into the night. I watched with fascination as my taste buds exploded with every mouthful of fry bread and vegetables.

I bedded down that night in my little tent with a full stomach and heavy eyelids. Peering out my tent flap, I could see the stars shining in the indigo sky and could hear the rustle of the people talking and moving about the encampment. My eyes could not stand the weight of their awnings any longer, and the sounds outside of my tent faded to a hum.

Before leaving the Sundance the next morning, I thanked my hosts and bid farewell. As I was walking back to my car, an old, gaunt man came up to me and took my hands in his. His skin was brown and wrinkled, his eyes dark bottomless pools, his face serene. He said to me, "You will dance one day."

Driving away from the camp on that early summer morning, I contemplated my continued inquiry into fear. What am I afraid of? Where there is fear one cannot experience love. Love is what we all seem to be seeking on this planet, myself included. Fear had cut me off from the one thing I craved. I had been living in a cocoon much of my life, trying to protect myself from being hurt, and in doing so, put up a barrier that would not allow love in. I was asleep, tucked away in my own warmth and security, and it was now time to emerge from the cocoon and fly. It was now time to wake up. I realized that I could not experience fearlessness until I first experienced my fear.

When we are bound by fear we cannot live our life fully. Acknowledging and working through fear can release us from its grip and enrich our relationships and experiences. So often in my past I "checked out" rather than be in the experience. When I had the opportunity to be in front of a group, I went through the motions and said the right things, but I wasn't home. My heart pounded, my knees shook, and I would disappear. Reflecting back, I see that I missed so much.

Sometimes we walk around as though we are asleep. We are tuned to automatic and become like robots. He or she did that, so I'll do this. He or she said that, so I'll say this. We become disconnected from our bodies. Our bodies are functioning—eating, sleeping, having sex, etc., and our minds are reacting to what is happening around us. Pinch yourself! Waking up is becoming aware. It is being aware of your feelings, both your emotions and your body. The body tries to tell us what is going on, it tries to let us know when we are operating on automatic, but we usually are not paying attention. Our minds are off doing one thing and our bodies are off doing something else. "Waking up" is waking up to our full capacity as human beings. Acknowledging the mind, the emotions, the body and the spirit.

Waking up brings responsibility—responsibility to how you want to live your life. It puts you in charge, therefore you are responsible for everything you do. It does not mean that you won't make mistakes. You will learn from all your accomplishments and mistakes. Your relationships with others will be more honest and open and less blaming. Instead of thinking "You made my life miserable," you might look at the part you played and the choices you made in any given situation. It may be that you need to leave the relationship in order to take care of yourself. Whatever the case, non-judgment of self, love of self and nourishment of self will help you to move beyond the (fearful) situation.

In order to acknowledge and open to the fear it was necessary for me to first open to love. Opening to love enabled me to make a connection with Great Spirit (God) which is love. The numbness was wearing off, I was waking up, and I knew it was time to experience my fear.

Exercise: *Waking Up and Connecting to Spirit*

Acknowledge your fears. Wake up and start *consciously* noticing how you are being in your life. Are you *fully present* in your day to day activities and relationships? Are you honoring your Self, expressing your ideas and feelings, aware of your body? Connect to the Self instead of running on automatic.

To feel a connection with Great Spirit, practice opening your heart center—opening to the flow of giving and receiving love. Close your eyes and imagine a sun rising in the center of your chest. As the sun becomes brighter, imagine that light extending out from you. *Feel* yourself open—*feel* the love and acceptance of yourself and others.

CHAPTER THREE

Reality Fear And Illusory Fear—Preparing For The Vision Quest

By dwelling in the past or fabricating
the future, we miss the moment,
the only real truth.

We trekked up a mountain in Boulder Canyon on a spring-like day in November. The day would be spent preparing for the vision quest that I would be doing in the spring. The first snow had not yet come, perhaps to give us time while Mother Earth was still warm and dry. Grandfather Sun was out in all his glory, generously spreading his warmth and brilliance over the land, and it seemed a perfect day to experience nature.

"Choose a place where you will feel comfortable," Raven suggested. I looked around and found a spot that permitted me a view of the valley below and the sky above. The space had a flat area where I could sit comfortably with a large rock for my back to rest against.

"Take this cornmeal and make a circle on the ground the size that you want," Raven offered.

I took the cornmeal from the pouch that Raven handed me and drew a circle in the earth from my pivot point in the center. There was enough room for me to sit against the rock and stretch my legs out fully. Raven threw her long hair over one shoulder and sat down in the circle with me.

She held out string and small brightly colored pieces of cloth—red, black, yellow, white, blue, green and purple, representing the seven directions. Her nimble fingers fashioned the cloth into bundles, each filled with a pinch of tobacco and fastened securely with a single piece of string, which linked one bundle, or prayer tie, to the next. When she had finished the prayer ties looked like tiny bright clothes pins strung across a miniature clothesline. Raven instructed me to pray to each direction with every prayer tie that I made, and then she got up with the grace of a swan in flight and stepped out of my circle.

"I'll be near by," she said, "Call me when you are ready to leave your circle." I watched as she made her way among the grass and plants, her hips swaying back and forth, her loose pale blue skirt moving in unison.

I looked down at the string and cloth. My awkward fingers worked to take each small piece of cloth in one hand and with the other place a pinch of tobacco neatly into the center. Painstakingly folding over the cloth and tying it with the string, praying to the directions, I busied myself with this task. Soon, I had a string of seven prayer ties and looked around my cozy space, not wanting to place them on the ground. I reached outside of my circle to pick up a stick and drew my hand back remembering that I was not to leave the circle for any reason. Instead of using the stick, I placed the prayer ties on several shoots of dried grass, then settled back against the rock.

"I'll take care of you," the rock person echoed. I felt safe and secure. I visualized my energy filling the little space. I looked around to see if there was anything sharing the space with me and spied a tiny ladybug, shiny black with red dots. This minute, active creature was using all her strength to climb up a mound of dirt only to find herself on her back and struggling to roll over and begin the climb once more. Without assisting the lady bug, I wished her success and decided to focus my attention on creating a ceremony in my space. I opened the rawhide medicine bag that hung from my neck and retrieved a handful of sage and cedar. I lit the sage and cedar and "smudged" using the smoke to purify my body, then laid the unburnt pieces on a small stone in front of me. The stone would act as my altar where I also placed other smaller, more colorful stones. This space became a very sacred place, and I felt a sense of home and belonging.

Time did not speak to me that day—only the trees and the wind. The trees became my friends, and there were so many there to help me feel happy and secure. Large pine, oak and cotton-woods towered over me from all sides and spread out over the hills and valleys like tall, strong sentries standing guard. A bird cawed in the direction of the South. I never saw it, but it continued to speak to me throughout the afternoon confirming my safety.

The wind visited me often and caressed my cheek with tenderness. It whispered sweet, soft sounds that words could only inhibit. The air smelled clean and fresh, unspoiled by man's pollution. I was in another world—a world of oneness with the things of Mother Earth and Father Sky. I was no better nor no less than all of nature that surrounded me. I felt relaxed and content, mesmerized, feeling that I was in a land of enchantment; that I was the bird that cawed in the distance, the ladybug struggling to make her way, the trees standing tall and strong and the wind whispering love.

Suddenly, a fly flew into my space, landed on my altar and then settled on my thigh. I couldn't believe it! I thought I was safe! That my space was filled with my energy protecting me and keeping out all others. The fly appeared very content on my leg, rubbing his feelers together, looking very smug as if he wanted to challenge me.

"Get out of my space," I shouted.

No movement.

"Why are you here? Get out!" Anger began to well up inside me, a grimace on my face.

Still no movement.

If a fly can get in so easily, I thought, so could a lion. I no longer felt secure and safe. I slapped at the fly, and he reluctantly flew out of the circle.

Moments later I called to Raven as I was anxious to tell her about the fly. This time she did not enter my circle but sat on the outside.

"Did you close the space that I broke when I left your circle?" she asked.

"No," I said, a little confused. "I filled my circle with light energy but did not specifically close the space where you left," I replied, becoming conscious that the fly had entered the circle at the exact place that Raven had broken when she left, and he flew out of the circle at the exact place where I had reached for the stick. Shifting my position against the rock, I listened for an explanation.

"When you lay the cornmeal," Raven explained, "you are creating a bubble of energy around your circle. When I left, there was a tear in the energy field. When you reached for the stick, your hand also made a tear. It is like a window shade that has been raised; you have to pull the energy back down and close it off. It is not enough that you filled your circle with light. You also have to repair the shield. The fly showed you that you were not safe and needed to do something more. Next time, I bet you will make sure your circle is secure, and listen for a message when you have a visitor."

This you can be sure of, I thought, as we made our way back to the car and the hustle of traffic on the canyon road. I did not want to return to "reality." I began to question what is real and what is illusion.

Reality fear is fear of what is real in the moment. It can be positive because it may be a threat to your immediate survival. Illusory fear is what we suffer from most because we rarely live in the moment. We live much of our lives in the past or in the future. We are often afraid of the unknown outcome of a thing or condition so we make it up.

There have been many hours in my life that have been spent worrying about what never happened. The nights I laid in bed wondering and worrying about my husband or children when they did not come home when expected. I wasted a lot of energy.

Realizing that my circle was no longer secure, I immediately feared what might happen, what snarling, wild beast might come and destroy me. There was no immediate threat; my mind had created one.

The experience in the mind can seem real and can stimulate a fear response. From seeing a piece of clothing draped over a chair in a dark room and imagining it is a monster to seeing your child in an auto accident when he or she does not return home on time, fear is a result, and it is all based on fabrication. This is where our neurosis lies. Living life in this way prevents us from experiencing the joy of the precious moment.

To stay in the moment I ask myself, "What do you know about the situation *now?*" When I answer this question honestly I know that anything beyond the information available to me in the moment is not real but rather an indulgence of my mind looking for an answer or result. Hanging out with the "unknowing mind" is the key to experiencing the present. It is the space, the void where we can touch the moment, and in that moment, everything can be new for the first time. It is like the slight pause between each breath we take. It is a moment of freedom.

Visualization: *Experiencing the Moment*

Close your eyes and imagine yourself in a difficult situation with a person close to you. Re-create the circumstances in your mind. Ask yourself what is happening *now*. Notice what you might be *making up* about the situation (what you make up is usually based on past experience). Notice how you are *reacting* to the situation (how you react is also usually based on past experience). What is fabrication and what is truth? How are you feeling in your body? Your body will clue you in on the answer. Take a deep breath and bring light into your body through the top of your head. Re-create the scenario in your mind again this time coming from what you observed as truth. *Choose* to communicate based on what is actually happening in the moment.

CHAPTER FOUR

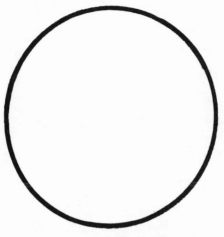

Fear of Death — The Coyote Story

Look to the circle, the spiral,
and you will understand life and death.

G randfather Coyote was a brave and determined fella moving swiftly through the forests
near Lyons, a small, unpretentious town close to
the foothills of the great Rocky Mountains north-
west of Denver. For many years he lived, mated,
had children and grandchildren, avoiding the
deadly hunter and man's traffic on the roads nearby.
He was a great hunter himself, bringing bountiful
kills to his family. At leisure times he stretched his
long, angular body on the earth and watched his
family feast and grow, the small ones frolicking, rolling and tumbling in the grass. As his offspring
became independent, Coyote moved on, becoming
a loner. He could then hunt for himself only and
rest when he chose. He was strong, clear sighted
and fast on his feet. Then Coyote grew old, he was
not as fast, not as strong and began to go blind in
one eye. He no longer could elude the hunter and
sometimes found himself near busy highways.

On a cold, grey day in late winter Grandfather Coyote took his last breath. He came to the highway and could not see as clearly, became confused, and in his wavering, came too close. He was struck, this old man Coyote, on his right side. His shoulder blade broken, he desperately tried to make it back to the safety of his homeland. He stumbled, faltered, his old body struggling to move on, the sound of traffic ringing in his ears, his strong heart that served him so well thumping hard against his chest. His days had been long and well spent. He now lay on the white bed of snow, his chest rising and falling, his breath labored. Light was turning to dark. He could hear the hoot of the owl from the direction of the forest as the human sounds began to fade. The chill of the wind ruffled his fur, and his eyes took on a glassy appearance. Sounds of the leaves dancing comforted him, and Moon Woman shined brightly above in the cold night sky. One paw inched forward, his body shifted. He laid his chin down into the blanket of whiteness, resting. A moment passed. Then, with one final lunge, his old body, coat still lovely with shades of brown and streaks of white, his long, fluffy tail trailing, lay still on the snow bank, all energy expended, all breath gone. Days passed. Grandfather Coyote, frozen in the snow, covered with ice crystals, waited.

I walked around to the back yard of Raven's house. She was there sitting on a large piece of clear plastic, head bent, busy at work with the "road kill." She had been wanting some coyote medicine when a friend brought Grandfather Coyote to her. Having been partially frozen, the coyote was well preserved. By the time I arrived, Raven had already removed the skin and laid it aside, working now to remove the flesh from the head and face. She would later boil the head to remove the remaining pieces of flesh and hang the skull in a tree to dry. Raven then planned to use it on a shield she was in the process of making. She used a small scalpel, cutting away bits of flesh being careful not to damage the bony structure. The feet had already been removed and were laid to one side. The scent of blood and other fluids filled my senses, and my stomach began to feel weak. My lesson today evidently was just to watch as I could not get my hands into the old coyote this time. Raven laughed at my squeamish ways and teased me with one of the eyeballs, saying it would make good medicine for me. I did not see the humor and was tempted to turn and go but knew there was a reason for my being summoned and decided to stick it out a little longer. I was definitely a city girl and had never seen a sight like this before!

As Raven worked, she dug out many small pellets of buckshot the old coyote had taken from the humans. I wondered how long he had carried them and if he had been in pain. Raven turned the carcass over and used a hand saw to open the chest and remove the heart. She cut the heart from its supporting arteries and held it up in her hand. It was beautiful, a work of art, with a rich deep, red color and darker purple/red veins moving up and branching out giving the resemblance of a tree.

"What will you do with the heart?" I asked, still keeping my distance but inquisitive at the same time.

"I will dry the heart, cut it up and give it to those who want coyote medicine for their medicine bag," she said, laying it gently to one side next to the coyote legs. "I'll use the brain to tan the hide," she continued. After keeping all of the coyote she could use, Raven took the rest of the carcass up to a mountain and laid it in offering to the wild animals. It is the Native American way to use all of the animal. In this way, old Grandfather Coyote is honored and thanked, and his medicine lives on.

His medicine lives on...what a beautiful thought. The coyote lived his life, lived his death and still lives on. Why is it that I and most of society have such fear of death? The more advances we make in science, the more we fear and deny the reality of death. We make the dead look as if they are asleep and keep the brain dead on life support when there is nothing more that can be done. I remember seeing my father in the hospital the night before he died. I could feel that his spirit was still present, and we had the opportunity to impart love to each other for the last time. The next morning I returned to his room to see an empty shell lying in the bed. I knew that it was not him. My sisters and I were grateful to his doctor who told us that he did not try to revive my father when his heart stopped as he knew that dad would not have wanted it. I was thankful that he was allowed to die.

One evening a few months after my father's death, my sister, Barbara, and I decided to do a hypnotherapy session to contact the spirit of my father and that of my mother who had died two years earlier. In the inner world my parents talked with me. Before I came out of the session my father told me that I would see him and my mother in the deer. When my eyes opened, I was looking at two large brass deer that had been a gift to them from me and were now sitting on my hearth. One deer was in an alert stance, his head raised to the sky and antlers majestically pointing upward. The doe looked serene as her head was lowered toward the earth. Sitting on my couch in a daze, feeling the warmth of the cozy living room and enthralled with the sight before me, I felt a calling to go up into the foothills near my home even though it was rather late and the night air was very cold.

My sister indulged me, and we both dressed warmly and hiked around the lake and up the hillside. We were running out of breath, yet I felt we had to go higher. At last, we came to a spot where we laid down on the ground and gazed at the stars in the heavens. She pointed out the Pleiades. We sat up and looked at the lights of the city below. I wondered why I had the need to be there after being with my parents. It occurred to me that I needed to view life from a higher perspective—from between heaven and earth. The deer were telling me the same thing. I could look down on the small cars, houses and landscape and know that there is more. I could look up into the heavens and feel that there is more. From my vantage point on the hill I could connect my spirit with theirs. The only thing that separated me from my parents was that our energy was now expressed in different forms. I began to see death as a transformation from energy and matter to another form of energy and matter.

We are literally being born and dying in every moment. Nothing is static—there is nothing steady that continues from one year to the next or from one moment to the next. Our bodies are constantly changing as cells die and are regenerated. We are never the same person from one moment to the next. We are made up of energy that never dies.

What we call death marks the end of the present experience. We came into the earth plane to learn and grow, and we only have a certain amount of time to accomplish our tasks in one life time. Moving from a state of life in the physical body to a state of pure energy is the ultimate in letting go. We leave behind the past which allows us to move into the spirit realm and to our next experience.

Exercise: *Seeing the Energy Field or Aura*

To get in touch with your energy field or aura hold out your hand against a solid light background. Gaze past your hand so that your focus is just beyond the outline of your hand. You may notice a white light of energy around the outline of your hand. Some people can see colors in their energy field or aura. To make this easier, try looking at your body in a swimming pool. Sit on the step of the pool or lean against the side and let your legs float in front of you. As you are holding on with one arm stretch the other out in front of you. Again, change your focus so you are looking just past the outline of your body. Look at the outline of your legs and feet. Look at the outline of your arm, hand and fingers. You may see several different layers of color swirling around your body. You may see color extending from the palm of your hand or the tips of your fingers. If you cannot see anything when you attempt this exercise continue practicing.

CHAPTER FIVE

Vaulting The Barriers Of Separation And Alienation—the Moon Lodge And The Giveaway

Separation gives birth to fear.

Close the gap between you and your world.

Everything is in relationship.

There are twin lakes near the place where I live and to walk there brings a serenity and peace far removed from the outside world. Bordering the lakes are large aspen, oak and willow trees with roots like fingers reaching down the bank to the waters edge. The lakes glimmer like two large glass plates reflecting the sun's rays. There is a path that winds its way around the lakes, first one, then the other in a circle eight. From the North side of the lakes facing West, the view of the mountains resembled a watercolor painting in pastels. Light, airy clouds shifted and moved repeating their pattern in the areas of shade on the landscape.

This was a perfect day to cut willow branches for the shields Raven would ask me to make during the year. I walked along the path immersed in the beauty around me. Grandfather Sun was shining his brightest in the clear cerulean sky, and a cool breeze gently moved through the trees transforming the leaves of gold and brown into many tingling musical chimes. The sun reflected on the water's surface in shiny, floating silver discs. Walking along the bank, I looked for a willow tree with long narrow branches close to the ground. The perfect tree lay ahead with its majestic branches raised to the sky and the long, lower branches inviting my approach.

I took out my clippers and cut select branches off the mother tree and sitting in the shade stripped the branches of their smaller appendages and leaves. I walked home pleased with myself, dragging seven naked willow branches behind me. The next day, my heart felt heavy because I did not acknowledge the willow tree by leaving a "giveaway." A giveaway is always important when taking something from the earth or another person. It is a way of honoring and saying thank you for the gifts you have received.

Two days passed, and I could not forget that willow tree by the lake. I decided to buy some tobacco and corn and go back to make my amends. A little tobacco shop on Pearl Street seemed the place to find the "right" tobacco that would be appropriate for my giveaway. I was in the shop for what seemed like hours sampling the different flavored tobacco and making sure the chosen flavor did not contain alcohol. The shopkeeper, a big, burly guy with whiskers, frowned and said that he did not know what the right choice would be. I finally used my own intuition and walked away feeling good about my gift.

Traveling on up Broadway to Alfalfa's Market, my mood was as though I was shopping for a special friend, a companion. I was able to purchase the last of the small blue corn of the season regretting only that it was still on the cob and would need to be patiently removed by me. Back in my living room, I sat for hours with the blue corn in the hollow of my lap plucking the kernels from the cob with a small, sharp knife and collecting them in a pouch. It was a meditative process, and I poured a lot of love into each corn cob that I worked on. Now, I was ready with tobacco and corn that would last me for months. The following day I sat out on the lake path with my offerings in hand, swinging my pouch back and forth as I skipped along. A voice resonated in my ears as I approached the tree. "Leave all of the tobacco," it said. It was not harsh or authoritarian, but I could tell it meant what it said. I took an offensive stance.

"No. I just bought this pouch of tobacco; it will last me a month for my giveaways," I replied stubbornly.

Again the voice echoed, "Leave it all!" I then realized that this was my lesson for not honoring the willow tree several days before, and I humbly gave up my meek attempt to defend my possessions.

As I stood in front of the willow tree, my heart soared. A warmth ascended upward from me and encapsulated us both. It was as though the tree were alive, in a way that we could communicate on the same level. "Forgive me for not honoring you during our first visit together," I said.

The tree just listened, branches swaying.

"Thank you for the branches that you have given me so that I may make my medicine shields and learn more about myself."

Again the tree was silent except for the crinkling sound of its leaves dancing in the breeze.

I opened the black leather pouch in my hand and spread all the tobacco around the base of the tree. Next, I took the corn and sprinkled it on the ground near the places where the branches had been removed. I stood back, took a deep breath and looked up into the billows of the rhythmic branches above my head. They were swaying delightfully, and I knew my new friend was pleased.

My experience with the willow tree marked a significant time in my life—a time that I began to view the things around me differently. What does this have to do with fear? It gave me a sense that we are all connected—not just as human beings but everything in our world. This would become more profound as I continued my journey.

Moon Woman shines her brightness upon us, reminding all women that we are sisters. I never knew what this meant before—sisterhood. I always felt a little intimidated by other women and have felt a competition with them. Now, I found myself participating in a moonlodge that Raven was having in my home. Twelve of us sat around on my living room floor waiting to find out what sisterhood was all about. A connection emerged between us as we shared our first moon time, the first of our menstrual cycles.

"I was twelve years old when my period started," I volunteered. "I was in the upstairs bathroom of the small, wood house we lived in, and sitting on the toilet, a warmness came from me. The stark, white tissue revealed a dark stain."

"I started!" I called out to any of my four sisters who might be near, only to find myself bewildered and alone. Finally my sister, Phyllis, came to the door and threw in a box of Kotex for me to use. That was it. I entered my womanhood without praise, without ceremony, without acknowledgment. It seemed like a curse. I recall fighting with the metal end of the sanitary belt so that it wouldn't make its way into the crease of my buttocks and cause pain. I was always shifting my position on the hard desk chairs at school. Others in the group also remembered those tenacious sanitary belts.

I was soon to find out that there is more that we as women have in common than the sanitary belt. Only one of the twelve women had celebrated her "right of passage" into her womanhood. In our society, most women are left feeling that their moon is their burden to bear. Instead, we were to learn that it is our most powerful time.

Because it is our most powerful time, we as women, can learn to be with this power in a good, resourceful way. Getting to know our body's cycle is a way to know ourselves. Communicating with our body helps to understand our needs, our desires and our pain so that healing emotionally, physically and spiritually can take place.

I surveyed the circle as each woman told her story. A profound sense of awe and admiration resonated within me. We of the sisterhood bring forth life to the planet. We give our blood and bear the children of the future. We are connected in a way that is sacred, and to be with each other in a sacred way, honoring our womanhood, is good. We can be loving and supportive of each other, and we can expand this love and support to all our sisters throughout the world. Our blood is not to be feared or be repelled by, but instead, to be honored.

Raven suggested that several of the women go into their backyard or to another private place in the outdoors and bleed into the earth during their moon time. It is a way of connecting with Mother Earth and facilitates healing in the body and emotions. Instead of wasting the unused fertility, we give it to the earth to use for her fertility. Bleeding into the earth in the darkness of night, connects Moon Woman and Earth Mother.

It can be very beneficial to keep a log of your cycle and also track where the moon is in its cycle. Notice when your moon begins and when it ends. The typical cycle of the moon and bleeding is the last seven days before the new moon; this is a quiet time when the bleeding woman has her strongest dream time and intuition. These are especially good times to record your dreams. The dream time can be a very powerful and insightful vehicle for knowing yourself better and receiving information to answers you are seeking in your life. Typically, the full moon is the time of ovulation which brings high energy when you are physically and mentally most alert. Your body has a wealth of stored knowledge and is waiting for healing that only you can give it.

Being in the moon lodge and acknowledging my connection with the sisterhood helped me to be with other women in a more intimate way; to know that we are not so different at the core of our being. Some may wear makeup, others not; some may dress fashionably, others in the simplest of attire; some of us are tall, others short and stout. We come in all shapes and sizes, some with large breasts, others with small breasts. It doesn't really matter, does it? Becoming a "sister" enabled me to let go of these insignificant differences. It gave me a space to be truly who I am and to be accepted. As sisters, we have a bond far beyond physical attributes. We can unite in a greater capacity. We can make a difference in the world we live in by embracing each other and becoming closer to our Earth Mother. In this way, we pave the way for all, men and women, to gain a better understanding of ourselves, each other and where we can contribute to healing the earth.

During this time, I also participated in a group of men and women who came together to connect, learn more about each other and gain understanding of the male/female relationship in our society.

The women told of being abused by men or taken advantage of by men in different situations. They shared the pain that they have endured with the men in their life; father, husband, brother, etc. Much to my surprise, the men told of similar happenings in their lives. Some of the men expressed anger that they have been blamed for all of women's pain in our society. They said that they have also been victims of our patriarchal society. Where women have been repressed in roles of subservience, men have been pushed to be all powerful, strong and responsible for succeeding in a career.

We heard men say that they have had a great burden placed on their shoulders and if anything, many felt powerless, without choices to meet the expectations placed upon them. They talked about maternal incest, some coming from a single parent home, being expected to take care of their mothers, to fill the empty space these women had inside. Most of the time it was emotional incest but sometimes also physical.

I was not aware that some men in our society feel powerless; that they too are victims. I began to bond with these men, looking into their eyes as they spoke of these things. I began to merge with them, male/female, and it became very clear that we need to work together to create a society where both sexes have a space to share their feelings with each other and work toward a common goal of allowing each other to be who we really are, or to find out who we are and support each other along the way.

With this understanding and willingness between men and women, we alleviate the pressures society has placed upon us and we on each other. We can only be innocuous when both sexes support each other in a new way. If not, we will continue supporting a system of separation and alienation that has been going on for hundreds of years. It is time for this to change, for male and female energy to come together in balance, so we can make choices that are free from stereotypical guidelines.

We can vault the barriers of separation and alienation by connecting to our physical environment and to each other. As we become closer, we can see that there is no separation between the earth and ourselves, between ourselves and others.

The first step in bridging the gap of separation begins with the integration of ourselves as male/female energy in the world in which we live. If we can honor both sides of our nature even though we are playing out a dominate trait in this particular life, we then will be able to honor the opposite gender, and when we can honor the planet that is holding us, we then will be able to live together in peace and harmony on the planet.

Exercise: *Closing the Gap Between You and Your World*

Work to bridge the gap yourself by respecting the things of the earth when you are in nature. If you take something from the earth, ask first for permission to do so. You will hear or sense the answer. Leave something in its place or give a silent thank you. Notice if you are taking a rock or a sprig of sage or anything else if there is an abundance in the area. If not, consider again if you want to remove it.

Also, you may want to expand your experience with groups so that you can learn about similarities among people, at the same time, respecting individual differences. Join a group of your own sex or a generic group that does not alienate male/female energy.

CHAPTER SIX

Nurturing Through Nature —
When The Dance Is Over

Standing on a rise above the plains I can see a gray,
heavy fog above the ground to the East.
It is not moving but seems to be stuck there.
Sometimes this happens in our relationships as well,
and we have to cleanse the air. So meet me up above the
clouds, up over the city and the trees and let's spend
some time together learning to Skydance.

S ometimes, in relationships, some of us go through many years of rocky times, happy joyful times, building a family, buying a house, getting two cars and two televisions. Eventually, it happens that we have learned everything we need to learn in the relationship and can just relax with each other for the rest of our days. Still, others learn all that they can from the relationship, and then it is time to move on, a time when the dance is over. These are the times when the dark clouds roll in, and we not only become out of step in the dance with our partner, but oftentimes cannot keep in step with our own individual dance of life. When we need to draw from our inner strength during this critical time, it is difficult to do. Our world may become stressful and fearful, wondering who is going to support us, who is going to hold us, who is going to help pay the bills, who is going to have sex with us, who is going to be there when we get home. We lose sight of the fact that we might be better off out of the relationship. We may be feeling a tremendous sense of loss, aloneness like we've never felt before, and we lose our strong, inner balance. When this happens we can become like a child looking for love, for nurturing, for approval and don't know where to find it. There comes a time when the dance with our partner ends, and it is just the time when we need to continue our own dance. And in doing so, we will attract another partner to dance with when the time is right. During the stressful time, however, the world of nature can support us.

A walk alone in nature is one of the most relaxing and nurturing things you can do for yourself when out of balance—taking in every little rock, every blade of grass; letting the plants, flowers and trees please the senses, hearing the crunching sounds that your shoes make with every step you take on the trail. Feeling Grandfather Sky above with all of his evening shades of pinks and blues and white; softness. Such softness right over your head. The feeling of being held by a strong mother and kissed on the forehead by the shifting, changing array of clouds in the sky above. This nurturing through nature supported me during a loss.

Some time ago, I deemed it necessary to leave a relationship that I had been in for ten years. It was a difficult decision to make but one I felt supported my own growth into the future. When a relationship ends there is sometimes an empty space left inside that needs to be filled in a healthy way. Perhaps there is anger, sadness and disappointment. To nurture and take care of myself, many hours were spent in nature in the foothills of Colorado. One particular evening comes to mind.

Summer had bid farewell. Shoots of dried brown grass mingled among the greener ones that were left. Flax was growing in abundance, and the evergreens sat steadfast, still sporting their dark, rich green leaves in contrast to the brown frailties of other foliage—the golden leaves of Fall. Peeking out among the grass were rose-like yellow flowers, the Evening Primrose. Bordering the West side of the lake, the cattails were standing tall and strong. Sage plants were beginning to dry up. There was a coolness in the air, and the water's glassy surface gave a surreal quality to the area. I passed a sign that read, "Give Nature a Chance."

The evening sky was blue, darker indigo clouds hung low, and clouds of gray, misty smoke lingered over the hills. I was up in those dark clouds. They were moving, coming very close to my dance space, and I felt that I was going to fall, that I could no longer contain myself since my recent loss. I might fall for a moment or a day or decide to keep dancing instead. I decided to dance through the dark, ominous clouds. Hearing the thunder beings rant and rave and roar, I got in touch with that part of myself that wanted to rant and rave and roar. That angry part of me that said, "It didn't work this time and I feel betrayed, I feel lost, I feel alone, I feel unloved!" I cried out, I screamed, I pounded on the mountains tops! I wanted to kick the rocks and tear branches off trees! I wanted to be as mighty as the thunder, and yet, I felt so small. In order to let go, I wanted to shake my body and feel the energy consuming me and tearing at my heart! I wanted to see it fly off my body into the sky and never return! I wanted the wind to blow hard, to blow through my hair, to blow and ruffle my clothes and blow away the energy that was keeping me feeling this way! I took a deep breath and allowed the wind to carry all of these feelings from me. I Let the tears flow as they needed to flow. Lighting flashed around me, and the rain poured down in torrents! It washed down into my hair and my face making it difficult to keep my eyelids open. The rain flowed down my body, to my feet, taking with it the anger I felt.

Then, I reached into the core of my being and knew that I was okay. I started moving, my feet came off the ground, spreading my arms, dancing in circles, gliding across the sky, dancing to the beat of the thunder beings. Moving in and out of that dark, gray mass and feeling once again that power source inside. Reaching over my head, screaming with delight; undulating vibrations moved through me. Feeling my strength, feeling again the love for myself. Being that love. Shouting as loud as I could so that my voice was booming throughout the heavens and across the plains!

In another part of the sky I saw a figure dancing also and knew the time would come again to dance with another. The sky was suddenly quiet, the clouds a misty blue. They seemed to be just lying above the ground like soft woolen shawls spread across the heavens. Two birds flew by, chirping. They looked so happy together and oh, so graceful as they circled each other and then moved away.

We need to find power and strength within ourselves so that we can come together in the dance of life where there is truly a creation of joy, of harmony, able to dance, able to flow, be free and be able to unite with another person. To be able to tap into, moment by moment, this power source within us will constantly feed our relationships as well.

Falling in love with yourself or another is doing the spiritual dance. It can be exciting as a sunset, an explosion of redness against the sky; feeling a profound sense of beauty and awe inside and giving that out to the other person. But what about staying in love? In order to stay in love with another, you have to stay in love with yourself. To keep the fire burning between you, you have to keep the fire burning within yourself. And once two people come together who have a good relationship and are ready to do this dance together, then they can begin to view life from a higher perspective, they begin to see situations and people from a spacious ground, and they can be as the eagle who flies above in the sky that is painted with colors that shift and change with every motion. They are ready to fly. They are ready to be above their little egos, above the pettiness of the everyday world, to begin to unite in joy from this higher place. To begin to skydance.

Exercise: *Cleansing The Air*

When you become more aware of your emotions and are able to express them, they become less likely to take control of your life. Find a safe place in nature, either alone or with someone to support your process. Take along a drum or rattle and use these instruments along with your body and voice to express how you feel. Give yourself permission to be totally uninhibited during this time using nature as a safe container for whatever you feel you need to do to cleanse the dark clouds in your life. Really use your vocal cords as a doorway through which you release tension from the body, being creative and giving yourself total acceptance. You will feel renewed and energized after your deliverance!

Give yourself quiet time, as well, to reflect, to think, to feel, to look at a big, yellow sunflower and say, "Hi, how are you doing today?" or "I'm not feeling so well." Maybe you will hear a message from the sunflower, maybe not. Look at the yellow petals—they are so bright, almost like parts of the sun's rays transposed. Look into the dark, brown center which resembles an eye, a door, a space to go and dream.

CHAPTER SEVEN

Accessing Personal Power—
Support of Spirits, the Inner World
and Altered States of Consciousness

There is a wealth of support within and around us.

All we need to do is to open to it.

I met my first spirit friends while walking at the base of the Colorado foothills one fall morning. I had reached a rise in the trail and could see Wonderland Lake below, placid, yet shimmering under the overhead sun, and I could gaze out onto the greenness of the plains and the stretch of mountains to the South. I was calm and at peace walking and occasionally looking at the ground to see if by chance a rock person called out to me that day. It was difficult for me to keep my eyes off the rock people—they each had something to say. Sometimes I would be drawn to one in particular and sit down with it in my hands, rubbing my fingers over the roughness, lines and hollow places. Closing my eyes and making an inquiry into an issue on my mind I would invariably get the answer by reading the markings on the rock.

Suddenly, I sensed someone walking with me.

On my right, I could *feel* a small Native American woman walking close by my side. She was petite, dressed in a brown buckskin dress and had long black hair plaited into braids that cascaded beyond her shoulders. She had a wispy smile on her lips, flushed cheeks and eyes like drops of black, shiny coal. To my left, I sensed a tall, lean, yet muscular man who seemed to move out from me in a dance like, playful fashion and then would return to my side. They both were young, light on their feet and vibrant with energy.

"Who are you?" I asked as I continued my walk.

"Little Crow and Big Brother," was the reply that entered my mind.

As time passed, I took many walks with Little Crow as she spoke to me words of love and support. She would be waiting for me on a rise above the lake, sometimes peering from behind a tree before she joined me.

"I am here to let you know that everything will be all right in your life," Little Crow said. "I know there is much sadness over the passing of your father, but he is in a good place, and you can still communicate with him in your inner world." My father had died recently from heart problems, and I was mourning his loss.

I could feel her sincerity and caring. Her spirit was walking joy, and I sensed that she came to uplift me. Although my sister and I had communicated with my parents under hypnosis, I was still feeling very sad and was now also worried about one of my daughters. Stephanie began having seizures several years earlier.

"Your daughter, Stephanie, will be all right also," she continued as if reading my mind. Her physical problem is not serious and she will overcome it."

"I will always be on this path if you want to meet with me," Little Crow told me. "But I will only be here, as I cannot come to you in your home at this time." I thought this to be strange, but it did give me the incentive to take more walks on the path. Rarely did I see Big Brother. Perhaps he found it hard to stay in one place for long.

Some time later, while walking this same path at dusk and holding no expectancy, I *sensed* the large head of a bear rise above me from behind. Shortly, and to my wonderment, a large figure of a Native American man peered out from under the bear head. His face took on the ruggedness of the hills behind us, his bronze skin taunt like stretched rawhide. The rest of the skin of the bear draped over his shoulders and around his body. He was massive in his stature and strength.

"I am your power and your strength," he said in a deep, growling voice and then faded away. I knew he was Little Crow's father, but I do not know how I knew this. His words struck me deeply and left a feeling within me of courage and love.

When I moved from that area of Boulder several months later, I thought I would never encounter this Native American family again. I was wrong.

Raven hovered over me as I lay on my living room floor. My friend and healer had brought sheep skin to cushion my body and a wool blanket to keep me warm. My eyes were closed, yet I could feel her presence, her energy near me. I could hear the flutter of the eagle feather as it moved the sage smoke across my body. My physical body seemed to disappear as Raven worked to deepen my trance. She called in any spirit helpers that would want to come in at this time to give me support and insight about my spiritual journey.

Little Crow came into my mind's eye. She just stood and smiled sheepishly, not saying a word. She was now wearing a white buckskin dress and hanging from her crown was a hawk feather. Then, I felt an omnipotent presence. Large. Strong. Powerful. It was the Native American man, Little Crow's father. I knew this was a powerful man among his people—a chief. He did not speak to me, but instead, started to dance around a fire. He was still wearing the bear skin head dress and robe as he held out his hand, inviting me to dance. I moved to where he was dancing by the fire and started to dance with him. My body began to vibrate. I felt powerful and my energy electrified as we began to move in unison. The feeling was one of freedom in my physical body and mind. We seemed to dance for a long time, moving around the flames, absorbing the warmth of the embers, feeling at one with each other. I felt honored that he would come to me and share his power. I knew that this was also my power, my strength. I could feel my chest expanding as I danced, my bare feet stomping the dirt of the earth causing dust to rise about my legs, my arms raised above my head holding a spirit staff of buffalo hide, eagle feathers and trinkets of turquoise and shells. Looking down at my body, naked except for a small piece of loin cloth; lean, strong and powerful, my eyes wide, hair billowing, I chanted to the heavens. I was not woman. I was not man. But both.

As the dance continued, losing my physical self in a whirlwind of energy, I connected to the lucid, flowing spirit that was me. This went on for some time until I once again became aware of my self and my surroundings. Reluctantly, I began to experience my physical body and found myself turning to walk away. The chief called my name and I turned and again faced him.

"This will make you powerful," he said, handing me a vial of green liquid. I drank the liquid and looked up into his deep, dark eyes; fell into them and was quickly transported through time back to the sheep skin on my living room floor. I did not realize until later when talking with Raven that I had taken bear medicine.

The bear is a strong and powerful totem and is located on the medicine wheel in the West. For me, the bear represents introspection, which is telling me to trust my own inner knowing, especially in the dreamtime; to listen to my inner voice that guides me during the waking hours. Bear medicine is fearless energy and at the same time, soft as a momma bear with her cubs.

I felt my power, my fearless energy; I tapped into the reservoir of gentle strength within me—a place where I go only occasionally, where another part of me takes over. I have experienced this when facilitating workshops. How wonderful it would be to integrate this power into other areas of my life, to live from this place, to let it influence my thoughts, behaviors and feelings. It is all right to cry, to feel unhappy or disappointed at times, but to have on the other end of the continuum a feeling of power and living consistently with it is how I wanted to live. Power is the opposite of fear; where fear limits, power is all encompassing, limitless, opening to potential and discovery.

"Thank you for this gift," I said to the chief as I opened my eyes. Raven was still sitting by my side, a little whimsical smile on her lips. I think she took the journey with me and was watching from behind a nearby tree.

An altered state of consciousness is another world apart from our conscious reality. It is a world where anything is possible, where healing can take place on many levels. It is also a place where our deepest seat of knowing can pour out exactly what is needed at any given time. How valid is this other state of consciousness? It is only valid as to how it manifests in your outer world. You will see that as change happens within, integration will happen in your life.

Your spirit helpers do not take the place of the knowledge and insight of your higher Self. Instead, they help assist you and support you in being closer to this higher realm. Your intuition will tell you if the information you are receiving is right for you. Your intuition is the voice of your higher Self. The more you integrate your mental, physical, emotional and spiritual selves the more clear your intuition will be.

Exercise: *Calling In The Spirits*
of The Seven Directions

In a standing position, face the direction of the
North and call in the gate keeper of that direction.
Ask for only the helpers that love you and honor
your free will. Ask for protection and guidance on
your journey during the waking hours and during
the dream time. Ask a specific question if you
desire before retiring, and you may get the answer
in a dream. Continue clockwise in a circle calling
in the other three directions, East, South and
West, returning again to the position facing North.
Call in Above, Below and Center asking for the
same protection and guidance. This can be done
anytime during the day or night. You can also call
in your higher Self and other spirit guides such as
angels and power animals. If you would like more
help with this, follow the visualization in chapter
12. Be aware that your helpers are available, and all
you need to do is ask.

CHAPTER EIGHT

Meditation—the Beginning of Fearlessness—the Prayer Stick

Watching the mind and how it works

can keep your thoughts from controlling you.

There is a freedom which pervades

when there is no longer attachment.

It is like coming out of a dark cave into a bright vista.

R aven and I walked up into the foothills at Chautauqua Park in Boulder in early March. Grandfather sun was shining, and the air was breezy. Since this was a weekday there were few if any hikers around the area. We stood looking out toward the plains and down on the city of Boulder at the base of the hill. I breathed in the cool, fresh air letting it fill my lungs and exhilarate me. We sat down on the dry ground side by side.

"Today you will take your first medicine walk," Raven said, "This time you will make a prayer stick. Focus on where you are on your journey, and pick up a stick that calls out to you, and pick up medicine objects that will be placed on your prayer stick. After you have completed the prayer stick, choose a tree and climb to a place in the tree and tie your prayer stick from one of the branches. You can come back to this tree to be with your prayer stick and meditate with it. It will give you insight and support as you walk this path." I had been feeling a little lackadaisical lately about my journey, and this was just the boost needed.

I set out on my walk feeling energetic and enthusiastic, focusing my attention on where I was on the Red Road. The day was beautiful and the pine trees cast shadows on the ground. A man walked by with his little black dog by his side. At last I was all alone, just me, the trees and the sky.

The stick was resting against a boulder and looked as though it were just waiting for me. It was about four feet long with several stubby appendages extending out from it. I picked it up and twirled it around in my hands like a baton. Raven's figure, sitting in the place that I had left, became distant and small. The forest around me began to close in as I felt captured by its beauty. I continued walking and came across a pine cone lying beneath a tree. Bending over to retrieve it, I experienced the feeling of my path as having many layers just as the pine cone does. I tied the cone on the stick with the red yarn from my pocket.

I weaved in and out among the many trees, stopping to sit on a rock and drink in the beauty and serenity around me. It was a little nippy so I kept my jacket on and my red cap snugly down over my ears.

Each tree I passed was appraised as if shopping for the special one in which to hang my prayer stick. I was continuously walking on dried, brown pine needles, so I reached down and scooped up a handful. Something will have to die in me on this Red Road, I thought. I tied the pine needles to the center of the stick. Within moments, I selected a tiny, yellow, dried flower to add among the pine needles. Something special will come out of this death I was told. As I turned in a circle among the many trees, my inner voice reminded me that I had not left a giveaway for the stick that I had picked up earlier.

Standing again before the boulder where I had taken the stick, I threw a palmful of corn with my thanks. As I turned to go back to the tree, an urge came over me to side track deeper into the woods to my right. I took a few steps and froze in my tracks! She stood just ten feet away, facing me, dark eyes piercing my soul. The wolf was large and beautiful; her fur thick, black and lustrous. Time stopped as we looked deeply into each other's eyes. What a magnificent animal! I immediately breathed in white light which filled me and became a halo around my body. For a moment, I envisioned a light around the wolf as well. As I turned to my left to leave her presence, she also turned to her left. I made my way hastily toward where the hill descends and stood on a boulder, Grandfather Sun beaming warmly on my face, my heart racing. A feeling of awe and wonderment pervaded me. Why would this wolf grace me with her presence? I did not know what it meant. I traveled the side of the hill, peering over the ridge for another glimpse of the wolf, but she was nowhere in sight. Looking ahead, I saw the tree where I would place my prayer stick.

Standing under the tree I felt the need to tie a giveaway bundle of tobacco and corn to the prayer stick, a reminder to me of giving more of my self, of being of service to others. Holding the prayer stick in one hand and using the other to support me, I stepped from ground to boulder to a lower branch of the tree and reached for a short protruding branch where I securely tied the prayer stick. I wondered if it was high enough so no one would disturb it. I thought of the wolf again and decided to take the prayer stick to the place where I had seen her and place it in a tree there instead.

As I walked back to that spot, my eyes searched the woods to the West, hoping that the wolf would show herself again, but she did not. I began to feel regret that I had not stayed with her longer; not tried in some way to communicate with her. I was so shocked to come upon her, I didn't seize the opportunity to stay with her for awhile. Yet, we had made contact. Why else would we meet? Her gorgeous, powerful presence touched me deeply, her dark, penetrating eyes, her thick plush winter coat, her sense of beauty and power and softness.

After choosing another tree and climbing to a safe height to tie my stick, I decided to sit in meditation for awhile. I went into the silence thinking I would hear her unspoken words, but I heard nothing. Instead, I felt a sense of love and tenderness and a boundless connection with all things. The wolf was a reminder for me to connect once again to that quiet place inside.

I was first introduced to meditation practice about

twenty years ago through the practice of yoga. My work at The Naropa Institute in more recent years has brought me back to the practice in a more profound and useful way. It is through the Buddhist teachings of mindfulness meditation that I will impart my experience of meditation to you. I draw from my own experience with mindfulness meditation, readings and teachings that I have been given over the past several years.

The practice of mindfulness meditation helped me to see more clearly what is happening in the present moment. Notice when you are not mindful, and you will see that your perception is narrow. Mindfulness is observing and experiencing without reacting.

In practice, just focus your attention on the breath. It is okay that the mind wanders. Just allow the thoughts to be there without attachment to them, and bring your attention back to the breath. The content of the thoughts become neutral so that you notice them and then let them go. There is a balance between being with the thoughts, letting them rise and fall and trying to do something. It is being relaxed and alert at the same time. Eventually the mind naturally slows down to a calmness, and you are free from struggling with your mind. We begin to see that thoughts are just thoughts, nothing more. It is only when we try to do something with the thoughts that there is a struggle.

When we are not mindful in our world, we accumulate habitual patterns that protect us from our world (both inner and outer). We repress our fears and other emotions. We project what we think is going on out there, and the more we panic, the more neurotic we become. This disconnectedness leads to hiding from ourselves, blocking our expression, withdrawing from others and becoming more and more self-conscious. We experience confusion between what is inside and what is out there. The louder the internal dialogue, the less we can hear what is going on. We lose a sense of our own presence and become caught up in being a victim of our world. When we disconnect, we block the flow of life and inhibit ourselves. We bind what is boundless and become our own prisoners. We end up with our bodies constricted, our thoughts running wild and our feelings bottled up or exploding. The more threatened we feel, the more rigid we become.

When we become mindful, we can notice what

we are doing—we can see how we react to things. We can then discriminate between reactions and feelings. We can only do this when we stop letting the ideas about our feelings obscure the feelings. It is important to be with and experience our feelings without judging them.

But what about the emotion of fear? There are times when we are really caught by it, when we identify with it. How do we remain conscious when we are caught up in fear? When we stop the chatter of the mind, we can start feeling more. We have to give up the attachment, drama and self-concern. We need to disengage from our relationship to the emotion and just look at the emotion itself. How does it feel in the body, in the emotions? See, feel the emotion in the moment without reacting to the situation.

Sometimes it helps to work physically with the emotions by stretching, moving or breathing. You can work with your mind by bringing in light along with more productive, expansive thoughts. Look at what is happening in your mind. Is it coming from a larger perspective, or is it just rambling, taking over your mental processes? We need to stop talking to ourselves in order to be in this higher perspective and start working toward calmness and clarity in the activity. This is mindfulness.

The more aware we become the more we can see how we cover things over, and as our clarity unfolds, we can continue to increase our awareness. Then, we can relax into being in the moment—letting go of a projected future, which is only a concept. When we can let go, we can become more open and expansive. This expansiveness, according to Buddhist teachings, is like an ocean, and if we open up we can begin to swim in this vast ocean of energy—spaciousness. In this space, we can handle all that comes our way.

In mindfulness meditation practice we begin to develop gentleness towards ourselves and appreciation of our world. We can begin to trust in the messages and feedback we get from our world which is always telling us what is going on and what is appropriate. We cannot listen if there is too much interference in our head.

There will come a time in our practice when the love and gentleness we have for ourselves can be of service in the world. We can have genuine compassion for others. As we experience that in meditation practice, we become more open to what is outside of us, and this feeling gives rise to fearlessness that anything external will be a threat or obstacle on our path. We begin to live our practice.

Exercise: *Meditations*

The following are ways I have learned meditation practice. The first, I learned while practicing hatha yoga and prajna yoga in the seventies. The second, I learned during my studies at The Naropa Institute. Try them both and chose the one that is best for you.

> (Note: Meditation does not have to be in a seated, erect position in your home. It can be walking in the woods or simply "being with" a tree or a flower or wherever you choose to focus your attention.)

Closed eye meditation - Find a comfortable place to sit, making sure your spine is straight. Place your hands in your lap or on your thighs palms up. Choose a mantra to use to bring yourself back to a state of quiet when thoughts arise. Example: "I am love." To capture the space of quiet and oneness practice "feeling" the meaning of words such as love, joy, peace, etc. instead of "thinking" them. When your mind wonders, bring yourself back to the quiet by repeating the mantra as many times as you need to.

Open eye meditation - Find a comfortable place to sit, making sure your spine is straight. Place your hands palms down on your thighs. Have your gaze extend out and down two to four feet from your body. Relax your shoulders and facial muscles and concentrate on your breathing. When thoughts arise, just allow them to be there and bring your attention back to the breath. Continue this process and the mind will eventually quiet.

You may want to construct an altar in a place in your home so that a special setting will be available for your meditation practice. It will also help to remind you to do your daily meditation practice. You may want to put some personal belongings or sacred icons on your altar; music, candles and incense is sometimes used. You can start out sitting for five minutes and increase the time as you become more familiar with your practice.

CHAPTER NINE

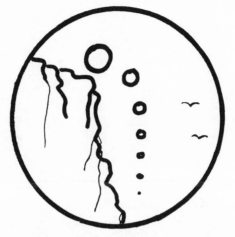

The Shield of Letting Go

*Letting go of something you don't have
is quite a mystery, but most of us have to look
at the concept anyway.*

We left the busy highway leading up from Boulder through the canyon to Nederland. I parked the Honda, and Raven and I retrieved four plastic grocery bags from the back seat. With bags in tow and our pockets filled with corn and tobacco, we ascended the trail which led high into a secluded, magical wilderness. As we trekked uphill, the earth came up to meet our feet; my breath already labored as the climb was steep. Raven climbed with zest and did not falter except to stop occasionally for me to rest. The ground was rocky, and we met weeds and dry grass along the way. Closer to the top, I began using my hands to push my knees down for each step. Reaching the top, breathing hard, I gazed across hills and valleys, mountains to the West and clear blue skies. Entering a different world from that of human beings, we came to a clearing and sat down. It was like a little nesting place encircled by boulders and trees.

Scattered on the ground we found bones and half eaten legs of the deer. It looked like a place where a wild animal came to enjoy his prey. My eyes took in the beauty of all that was around me—the trees, rocks, and plant life seemed to become communicative. Birds flew in and out of trees and called their welcome to us.

Raven turned to me. "We are here for you to take a medicine walk so that you can collect symbolic objects for your first shield. What would you like to work on?" she asked.

"Fear has always been an issue in my life," I said, "fear of losing those I love, fear of death. I would like to let go of fear."

"So your first shield will be the Shield of Letting Go," Raven said, a serious expression on her face. "You will take your walk alone. Focus on your issue of 'letting go'. Pick up those things you are drawn to, and in their place leave a little corn or tobacco depending on whether the object is feminine (corn) or masculine (tobacco)."

I looked around this beautiful but unfamiliar place, hesitant to do my medicine walk without Raven.

"If I see you or you see me, we'll look through

each other," she said.

Leaving the safety of our space together, I entered an unknown arena where nature played center stage. The wilderness beckoned me, and although I felt some fear, I was drawn in by its seductive lure. What if I encounter a hungry lion, I thought. All of a sudden I felt a peace inside and heard the lion say, "I won't come out today, you're not ready for me yet."

I walked on, waiting for a strong pull from nature. I looked down and saw a white rock shaped like a heart with a crack down the center. I had been through a lot in the past years, and my heart had been wounded. I had become a wounded healer; feeling what others feel and helping to facilitate their healing also. I bent over to pick up the rock, my hand clutching its hard, smooth surface.

"This is my heart that has been broken yet is still strong," I said to myself as I put it in my medicine bag, leaving a pinch of tobacco in its place.

I ventured out into the wilderness and up hills forgetting time. I looked down at the earth again and staring back up at me was a piece of bark from a nearby tree. It looked like a mask with frightful features and an all-knowing eye in the center.

"This is my fear," I said, dropping both corn and tobacco on the ground where it laid. I hastily added it to my promising collection.

I passed numerous animal droppings on my walk but just stepped around them. Next, I came upon a beautiful evergreen bush which grew low to the ground. It seemed to stand out in all its bright, green glory in the mist of the brown earth.

"You represent my children," I said to the evergreen. "You are somehow letting me know that they are all right, and I need not be concerned or fearful for them. You are bright and colorful, never dying which is like the love I have for them. They have their own power, and I can honor that by standing back, letting them live their lives and be present to support them if they ask. I bent down and gently removed a branch. "Thank you," I said as I felt a surge of love radiate in my breast while placing a palmful of corn at the base of the bush.

Shortly after my enchanting encounter with the evergreen, I spied a family of sage, soft colors of grey/green that huddled together in clusters. I knew strongly that sage would need to be a part of my medicine, so I gathered a handful and left behind corn, intuiting that it was feminine sage. I could feel the feminine in me, knowing that my personal power as a woman is to walk tall, be confident, creative, productive and to help other women tap into their power also.

Feeling complete with the day's gathering, I was ready to return to the place where Raven and I started. I stood and looked in all directions. A panic arose as I realized that I did not know which direction to go. As my eyes searched the emptiness, I saw Raven walking about thirty yards away. She looked completely akin to the area as she moved with the flow of the land. I wanted to call out to her and get help in finding my way back, but remembered her words, "If I see you or you see me, we'll look through each other."

I tread ahead alone searching for the clearing where we had begun our day. I could not recall the markings of trees or boulders. Several times I came upon a place that looked like the right one, but noticed there were no bones of the deer scattered about. I began to feel more discomfort. What if I remained lost? Night would be encroaching soon. The afternoon was fading fast and dusk was descending all around me. I looked down and saw a piece of dried wood that looked like a bird. My hand reached for it almost as if I had no say so in the matter. My lips seemed to move involuntarily.

"Show me the way," I implored the birdlike branch in my hand. As I began again to draw on my intuition, I walked for a moment and thought "too high, go down the hill." Walking in one direction, I heard, "No, go in the other direction." Words came like clear thoughts in my mind as if I was communicating with this bird shaped stick in my hands. "If you find your way, you can have a bone," it said. I could not phantom the idea of wanting a dirty, blood stained bone, but the words sounded like an honoring so I did not question them.

A few minutes later, I saw the spot. Raven was already there sitting, legs crossed, her thick braid tied in thongs rested over one shoulder. She looked serene and at one with the wilds. I had found my way home.

I exuberantly approached, my legs carrying me saliently to the clearing. Pleased with myself I laid the birdlike stick down with many thanks and chose a bone to add to my treasures. I settled down next to Raven in the moist earth and dried pine needles.

I spread my collection before us: the heart shaped rock, the bark, the evergreen, the sage and the deer bone. Time was taken to share with Raven the meaning of the objects, and then she, wearing a sheepish grin, began to speak. I have seen her playful energy before and learned to expect anything during these times.

"I have something for you to add to your medicine," she said with a huge grin and a sparkle in her eyes. "I had a feeling that you came across it many times on your walk, but I knew you would not pick it up." She was holding a closed fist and asked me to hold out my hand. I did so timidly. Raven dropped a few light, small objects into my hand, and with great curiosity and trepidation I looked into my palm to find three tiny rabbit droppings.

"The rabbit represents fear," she said, "If a rabbit freezes out of fear, the only way he can run is to shit. He has to let go of fear and run, or he will be hunted and killed. This is a humble reminder to continue letting go of fear."

I felt the truth of what she said but could not imagine rabbit droppings on my shield. As if reading my thoughts, Raven chuckled, "When something is true for you it is beautiful. Your judgements of bad and good, ugly and beautiful are based on social programming. As you walk the Good Red Road, you will learn to determine what is true and therefore beautiful for yourself."

Raven told me her version of a story she had read in a book by Lucia St. Clair Robson:

There was once a very brave young man whose father took him on his first buffalo hunt when he was fourteen. The young man was very excited and charged into the herd, firing an arrow into the heart of a huge bull. As the bull charged, the boy's horse turned sharply, and the boy fell off his horse just as the buffalo fell on his side, nearly drowning the boy in a gush of piss. The boy was so full of adrenaline, he jumped back on his horse, charged back into the herd and fired another arrow. This arrow flew with such force that it went clear through the body of one buffalo and into the heart of another, killing them both. When the hunting stories had all been told, the hunting chief called for a special naming ceremony for the boy. "Buffalo Piss is great hunting medicine for you, my son. So, for as long as you are a great hunter, your name shall be Buffalo Piss." The young man was happy and honored to have been accepted into the Hunting Society at such a young age and for receiving a true and meaningful medicine name which he carried until his death.

Raven laughed at the look on my face. I loved the story, but hoped that I would not receive the medicine name of "Rabbit Shit." With Raven as a teacher, I wouldn't be surprised!

When I returned home I laid all of my medicine out before me on my living room carpet and was anxious to begin the creation of my Shield of Letting Go. I had added to my collection a small feather found near my home and a purple, dried flower and two leaves that had fallen from a tree in my yard, one of gold and one of bronze. The dried flower represented to me the purple of the crown chakra (one of seven energy centers in the body); opening to the spiritual and to the higher Self. The gold and bronze leaves became a cycle of time with no beginning and no end—we are as the leaves as we are born, change, die and return again.

I bought a piece of white rabbit fur from a local hardware store and attached it to one of my hoops. Next, I placed the medicine objects. The piece of bark (fear) clung to the left side of my shield looking very threatening next to the evergreen. The rabbit droppings were spaced where they skipped across the shield from the bark to the center where new life and joy begin to appear. The heart shaped rock I placed in the center, and the feather went at the top of the shield as the dried flower, the leaves, the sage made their way clockwise around the shield.

Standing back and looking at what I created, I was captivated. I could see how fear kept its eye on the beautiful things in my life—my spirituality, my emotions and my choices. It was time not to allow fear to govern my life any longer, and I would be reminded of this every time I looked at and meditated with my Shield of Letting Go. To let go, I needed to be willing to forge ahead in all that I did, breaking the bond with fear. The deer bone hung from the bottom of the shield to remind me that I am more than these things—that what is in physical form perishes, but what is in spirit form never dies.

Later, I moved the evergreen representing my children from where it was placed next to the bark (fear) to the opposite side of the hoop. I accomplished putting some distance between fear and my children, so the shield, like my experience, was already transforming.

When I experience "letting go" I can feel a burden has been lifted. It can only be explained energetically—as though my body becomes lighter. During a fall semester at Naropa, I walked by a teacher on campus after letting go of a relationship of many years that I knew was unhealthy for me. The teacher stopped me and commented that I looked lighter than I did the previous semester. I said that I felt lighter but was surprised that it was physically noticeable. As we let go of the burdens we carry, we not only feel better, our energy is lighter as well.

Visualization: *Letting Go*

In addition to the visualization below, consider collecting "medicine" objects from nature and building your own personal shield. To make your hoop, soak the willow branch in a tub of warm water until it is pliable enough to bend into a cir-cle, overlapping the ends and tying it together with string. The hoop will then be ready to decorate as you choose.

Close your eyes and imagine that you are in a magical garden. It is a place that only you can go. As you walk into the garden you can see brightly colored foliage of various colors of green and yellow. The ground is covered with flowers and ferns and the sky overhead is pale blue with fluffy white clouds floating by. You can see different species of birds, their feathers every color of a rainbow. As you are walking through the garden you come across a sparkling pond, the water inviting your entry. You take off the clothes you are wearing and discard them, and you wade into the cool, refreshing water. Submerging yourself in the water you can feel your body becoming renewed.

There is a waterfall at one end of the pond and you go now and stand underneath it feeling the water pouring over your head, neck, shoulders and body like luminous liquid light. You can feel all the negative history your mind and body has accumulated being washed away. You relax, surrender and allow this history to be carried down a stream and away from you. Getting out of the water and standing on the bank, you feel new, clean and vibrant. Raising your arms overhead, you sense your power and your strength. You put on new clothing—anything that you feel comfortable in. Now open your eyes. You can do this visualization as often as you feel the need.

CHAPTER TEN

Going Beyond Fear— the Sweat Lodge

Let us touch the earth

and hear our cries turn into song.

On a hot day in September I joined a small group of volunteers, and we worked all day clearing the land at the Buffalo Ranch so that we could rebuild the sweat lodge. Raven knew the ranch owner, and he gave her permission to use his beautiful land for our ceremonies. The land was a disaster. Tall grass and weeds grew everywhere; sage was tall and willowy and ready to be picked. There were about ten of us, men and women, working together as a team, cutting grass, bending over to pick up bundles and carrying them to a pile nearby. We worked hard under the hot sun, and we needed mouthfuls of water regularly. The land was dry and dusty; my clothes and hair stuck to me like an unwanted second skin. Long, sweet smelling sage was picked by the armfuls and stacked near the soon to be refurbished altar. We made sure all the sage plants received a sprinkle of corn, and their roots were left in place in the soil so they would return once again in the Spring.

We took a break around three in the afternoon and sat on old, soiled blankets and bedspreads that had been taken off the disassembled sweat lodge. It had caved in on one side from the wear of the weather and invasion of animals. We all ate vigorously, devouring peanut butter and jelly sandwiches and other snacks we had brought from home. It was good to work for a common goal. There was a sense of community here that I had never felt anywhere else. Working on the land, being close to Mother Earth affirmed that we are all her children preparing her for ceremony to give us rebirth.

We completed preparing the earth just before dark, Moon Woman's face was already looking down on us. We had worked many long hours building the sweat lodge and were all exhausted. Long, agile willow branches were chosen for the poles of the lodge, twelve in all. They created a sturdy structure which held the carpet, blankets, spreads and plastic that covered them. A hole was dug in the earth in the center of the lodge to hold the stone people, which were heated in the fire that was blazing in the fire pit. As night fell, the air turned cool, and the warmth of the fire was comforting.

Building the fire and heating the stones is a sacred ceremony in itself. A platform of wood is built on the ground inside the pit. The stone people are placed on this platform. The first seven, which are offered to the seven directions, are placed first, each honoring the seven directions. The remainder of the stones are then placed upon these and more wood is set in teepee style over the stones. The fire is lit underneath the platform which allows the entire structure to be in the path of the flames. It cooks the stones for several hours until they are ready to be brought to the lodge and placed in the lodge pit. Each of the first seven stones are blessed as they enter the lodge, then the remaining stones follow.

The door of the lodge is closed, and prayers and songs are offered while the hot coals are given water. Steam, moist and penetrating, filled the air in the lodge. My skin became damp and my lungs took in the humidity. We were doing four rounds using forty-four stones. Each round honors the four directions, North, East, South and West. Between rounds, the lodge door is raised and outside air is allowed in.

I sat in my place in the lodge with my towel

under me and an extra towel to put over my face to protect it from the steam. My lungs had been congested for several days. "Great Spirit," I prayed, "I ask for a physical healing tonight. Please send in your spirit helpers to enter my body and clear my lungs so that I can breath freely."

The steam went deeper into my lungs with each breath as I sat in an upright position with my legs folded in front of me. My dress had become drenched, and my hair was dripping tiny droplets of water around my face.

I could feel the presence of the others in the lodge with me; a safe feeling among kindred spirits both of the physical world and of the spirit world. Great Spirit's presence filled every inch of the sacred space from wall to wall.

I looked around in the darkness of the lodge and listened to Raven sing prayers and acknowledgment of our reverence and respect for Great Spirit. Feeling the urge to be closer to Mother Earth, I put my hands down to feel the cool earth and spontaneously rubbed the dirt all over my arms, legs and face. It felt cool and nurturing. Feeling as though the lodge was the womb of the mother, I lay down, moving my towels to one side and letting the earth cradle me in her bosom. I felt sadness in my clinging, my innermost being remembering the lack of nurturance from my childhood. Darkness. Dampness. Coolness. Earthiness. I was alone in the deep recesses of the earth, being held by her, loved by her and protected by her. The smells were earthy and clean that entered my nostrils, and my body felt small and enveloped by a strength and force that I can only attempt to describe. My eyes searched the dark corners of the lodge, but I could only feel. I was a babe again in the arms of the mother, able only to simply be, taking in all the warmth and love she bestowed upon me. Being cleansed, having my pores open, releasing toxins and negativity from my body, breathing in the steam from the rock people, purifying, I was preparing for a rebirth.

By the end of the fourth round, the rock people began to cool down and a gentleness pervaded the lodge. Gentle arms surrounding, soft kisses on my brow, I felt the mother rocking me into dream time, but I did not sleep. When it was time to leave the lodge, I did not want to leave my curled up position enfolded by this serenity and love. The earth spoke to me in this way.

Stepping out of the lodge into the cold of night my skin tingled, my feet planted on the earth I gazed upward at the many sparkling stars flung across the night sky. Tip toeing over to where I had left my street clothes, and noticing that my lungs had cleared, I hurriedly changed out of my wet sweat clothes and into my dry but not yet warm ones. I felt reborn, coming out of the mother, bursting forth into a new day. I felt hungry, yet nourished.

I got a ride home with two friends, their old pickup making its way lazily toward Boulder on the straight stretch from Lyons. We were all weary yet content so few words were spoken. The foothills took on Moon Woman's glow, and the mountains behind were awesome, yet soft and retiring. Boulder lay ahead, the lights of the city twinkling as if playing back a tune from the night stars. Ready for my pillow, I snuggled with my friends in the closeness of the front seat of the pickup.

I soon found myself back home, looking in the bathroom mirror, covered with caked dirt from the top of my head to my feet. What a sight! It was two o'clock in the morning and I felt wonderful. I jumped in a hot shower and into bed where I fell asleep quickly after the long day's adventure.

Being close to the earth in such a profound way moved me to experience something beyond fear— a feeling of total safety and nurturance. Perhaps many of us did not get the nurturing we needed in our past. We cannot change our perceived child- hood experiences, but we can find ways as adults to nurture the child that we have inside.

It is an experience of acceptance, of trust, of integration, of oneness. The wonderful realization is that this is always available to us—this connec- tion to Mother Earth. For the first time, I was con- nected to heaven and earth—I was their child.

Exercise: *Connecting With The Earth*

If you have the opportunity to participate in a sweat lodge ceremony you may find it a healing experience. Make sure the person who is leading the sweat is qualified to do so. If it is not possible to attend a lodge try the following exercise instead.

Find your own place in nature. Sit on the ground and put your hands in the soil of the earth. Feel Mother Earth supporting you. This experience brings a sense of peace and stability. If you have the urge, lie down, close your eyes, and feel Mother Earth holding you. If you feel like rolling or rubbing the dirt over your body, allow yourself this freedom.

CHAPTER ELEVEN

Outrageousness— the Vision Quest

Here I am, standing naked, a tiny speck
in a vast wilderness, but I am not alone.

R aven and I stepped from the moist heat of the sweat lodge out into the cold dampness of May. It had rained all day and the ground was saturated. The late afternoon air held a mystic feeling as I gathered my prayer flags and prayer ties and walked with Raven to set up my circle for my vision quest.

A vision quest is a sacred ceremony between a person and Great Spirit. Deciding to do a vision quest is a huge commitment in letting go. You become completely vulnerable, and this is where trust in yourself, your higher Self and your relationship with Great Spirit is truly tested. It is a time of surrender. It is a time of utilizing all that you have learned and experienced in nature and in the spirit world. It is a time when you are connected to your emotions, your body, your mind and your spirit. This connection within yourself connects to everything in your world, and you know that you are not alone. It can be done alone or it can be facilitated by a person or a shaman who has made a commitment to be of service in this way. This support person stays a distance away, prays for you and keeps a psychic connection with you. They focus on you and your safety and you focus on your connection to all things, seeking your vision.

I began to prepare weeks before for my vision quest, purchasing my vision quest brown wool blanket and my dress, making my prayer ties and flags and endowing each with a prayer. Prayer flags, like prayer ties, are prayer bundles filled with tobacco and prayers. They are tied on poles about 3-4 feet high and represent each of the seven directions. Each flag's color corresponds to the color of each direction: North - white, East - yellow, South - red, West - black, Above - blue, Below - green and Center - purple.

I, along with six other women, sat in the sweat lodge to purify before going to our individual vision quest spot. Most of the others were already settled in their circles when Raven and I walked from the encampment toward my spot, which Raven had chosen for me. Raven suddenly engaged me. "Repeat after me, 'I have no name', and continue saying those words until you really mean it," she said. I glared at her in bewilderment but did as I was asked.

"I have no name," I said, feeling a certitude after saying it only once.

A third of the way to our destination, Raven stopped and turned to me again. "Repeat, 'I have no face'.

"I have no face," I said, as though I was giving up my identity.

We walked another third of the way and Raven became still again. "Now repeat, 'I have no family'." I swallowed hard not wanting to say this. I felt like I would be giving up my family and I ached inside. I closed my eyes and felt them become wet. "I have no family," I whispered, voice trembling. I cleared my throat and said more clearly, "I have no family."

We walked the final steps of the journey to the spot where I would set up my vision quest circle. Raven turned to me and said, "I have no purpose." I looked at her and felt naked and alone. My clothing had been stripped away, and I was exposed in a raw and indigenous way. "I have no purpose," I repeated.

"Louder."

"I have no purpose," I echoed.

It was important that I give up the things I identified with and seek my vision without attachment. Giving up attachment was not a new concept for me, but it had been a struggle all my life.

Reaching my spot took some maneuvering across a stream, its edges bordered by tall grass. The water rushed over and around rocks as though it was in a great hurry to reach some unseen destination. Swishing and gurgling as it passed, it seemed to pay no attention to my dilemma of crossing it. Raven jumped from rock to rock in her agile, confident way, touching down to spring up again. I followed her lead, my long legs spread wide for the jump. Like a ballerina on a slippery stage, I lost my footing and fell into the icy water. My boots, wool socks, and the bottom half of my sweat dress and my prayer ties were soaked. I quickly got up wondering why Great Spirit was already making things tough for me.

There was nothing to do but continue the journey. Raven helped me, and I set my flag poles in each of the seven directions into the soft, wet earth near the side of the stream. I enclosed my circle by wrapping the long string of prayer ties from one pole to the next until all the string was used. I spread my blanket out in the center of my circle and placed my drum and medicine doll on a lump of dirt near the south flag pole. Raven squatted outside my circle and said a prayer for me. She asked Great Spirit and the spirit helpers for my safety and that I would receive the vision I needed. After assuring me that she would be at the fire pit and that I could call her at any time with the beat of my drum, she left. Raven would maintain a psychic connection with me throughout the quest.

There I was standing in my circle on wet ground, with wet clothes and only a blanket. I had brought an extra pair of cotton socks and leggings so I quickly changed into them, but in the damp chill of this May day, they could not take the place of my boots and wool socks. Sitting on my blanket, I gazed around me, acclimating myself to the terrain. It was a beautiful spot—hundreds of tiny, yellow daisies were scattered over the damp, green clearing. The flowers were so bright they looked like stars that had fallen from the sky and embedded themselves in the earth. The area around the clearing was thick with trees and the melodious sound of the stream was like music to my spirit. Large, cumulus clouds, like clusters of cotton balls, floated in the blue sky. I stood facing each direction and prayed to Great Spirit. I sang several Lakota songs and chanted. Just before dusk, the thunder beings decided to make themselves known. Clouds, dark and ominous, gathered together forming balloons of smokey grey. The sky rumbled as if God were a giant stomping around the heavens, and the vulnerable earth shook beneath Him, but no rain fell.

As I continued to pray and sing, darkness rolled in like a shade pulled down across the cloudy sky and gently enveloped everything. I lost track of time and finally laid down to rest. Moon Woman emerged at her fullest from over a mountain top and slowly moved across the night sky. My body became very cold, and as I clung to the damp ground, curled up in a fetal position, I became aware of a grunting sound. I thought, oh God, there must be a bear nearby! I could not tell the direction from which the sound came but suspected it was behind me, to the West. My body began to shake! I was afraid that if I opened my eyes and turned in the direction of the West I would see a huge, black bear standing on hind legs rushing toward me! Soon I was shaking uncontrollably, and the frigid night air penetrated my bones causing an ache down to the marrow. My eyes narrow slits, I peeked out, afraid of what might be lurking in the depths of night. Moon Woman was now high and lit up the darkness like a beacon from a lighthouse. I could see them clearly across the stream. Three buffalo had come to visit, and the largest one was drinking from the stream. The sight comforted me, yet I could still hear the grunting from behind.

I could freeze in my fear, letting my imagination run wild, or I could choose movement, clarity and understanding of my situation. I stood in my circle in the middle of the night and pounded my drum. Surely, if there was anything threatening nearby it would soon scamper off. I saw Raven jumping the stones over the stream, and she came to me with ease and unconcern on her face. I told her of the cold and of the grunting noises, my teeth still chattering as I poured out my fears to her.

"The grunting sounds you heard were from the mother buffalo calling to her child," Raven explained. "Out here it is difficult to tell where sounds come from as they bounce off the surrounding mountains. Your clothes are still wet so come down to the fire pit and get warm," she continued. "I am very tired so you can tend the fire while I rest for a while." I agreed and we walked together back to the encampment. Looking up at Moon Woman, I guessed that it was between four and five in the morning. Raven went in her tent for a nap and I tended the fire, adding new wood and stoking up the cinders. After tending the fire for a couple of hours, with my hair singed and beads of sweat on my brow, I appreciated what a responsibility it was. When Raven returned to relieve me, I crawled in the back seat of her car where I caught an hour of sleep.

The morning brought blue skies and the warmth of the sun and much thanksgiving. I went back to my circle and decided to sit in each of the directions and just take in the beauty around me. The South honored me with hummingbirds. They were fascinating to watch as they fluttered up into the air and then made dives toward the ground. They told me that it was time to have love and joy in my life. The West brought me a tiny fly whose message was to give up negativity both in my own thoughts and in relationships that supported it.

As I looked toward the North, four eagles flew out from behind a mountain peak. Two veered off to the West and back behind the mountain and two did an eloquent sky dance together, right before my eyes. I sat in awe, knowing that the eagle is a powerful totem in the Native American tradition. I was honored that the four eagles came and graced my presence. They supported me getting in touch with my own power, ability to soar and wise inner knowing. I shifted my seated position to face East and spied a tiny lady bug crawling up my East flag pole. She was slow but determined as she inched her way up. When she reached the edge at the top of the pole, she clung to it for what seemed like forever. I urged her onward, "Come on, you can do it. You can reach the top," I said. Another move and she was sitting on top of the flag pole. I am that little lady bug, I thought, and I can reach the top—my potential, my goals, my higher Self. This was a day that I was extremely grateful for all the gifts I had received.

That evening, I left my circle to join the others for another sweat lodge ceremony. As I stepped over my prayer ties, my foot got caught and one of the strings broke. I was devastated! Now my circle would not be safe, I thought. It had been broken, and I got a feeling that it was not a good idea to spend another night in it.

We met with Raven at the fire pit before entering the sweat lodge. I told Raven what had happened when I left my circle, and she said that I should honor the message I had received. In the sweat lodge, a woman told of a visit from a black bear. She had seen a black bear as it approached her circle. It stopped about ten yards away and sat near a tree. The woman crouched low against the earth, her heart racing from fear. The bear and the woman faced each other in the stillness for a long time, and then the bear turned and lumbered away. Another woman told of a visit from a mountain lion. A beautiful, golden mountain lion came and sat just outside of her circle. Just before dawn it got up and scampered off into the hills. I did not share my visit from the eagles as it suddenly felt insignificant compared to the other stories told. Their night visitors came so close to them, and they managed to stay grounded and in their circles. I wondered what I would have done. My vision had taken place in the sky far from a threatening advance on the ground. My thought subsided as I brought my attention to what Raven was saying.

Raven told the group that she had also gotten a strong message from Spirit that we were not to spend the night in our circles. Instead, she said, we would spend it by the fire pit.

That night, a raw coldness fiercely descended upon us. Even lying on the bank around the fire pit did not keep me warm. It was too cold to sleep, so I lay there and prayed for a vision.

An eagle flew over my head and landed on a rock near by. I thought, how could I be dreaming when I am not even asleep. I noticed that the eagle landed closer to one of the other women, and I felt jealous. The eagle told me that I should not compare my experience to anyone else's—that my vision was just as important and powerful as any other. I did not realize how true this was and how blessed I was for such a great and powerful vision. As the earth was bathed with light once more I wondered if I had slept and dreamed or if I had been awake all night. There did not seem to be a distinction.

On the final evening we were to decide whether to make a commitment to do a vision quest each year for four consecutive years. I sat in my circle again on the last day contemplating my situation. I do not have time to make such a commitment, I thought, and I am not ready for it. As I struggled with my mind, clouds covered the sun, and it began to rain. I put my decision on hold, took my drum in hand and sang and prayed for the clouds to roll back and let the sun shine through. To my amazement that is just what happened!

As I settled back down on my blanket large hale stones started to fall from the sky. They bounced off my body and the ground like popping corn hitting sizzling oil. The sudden changes in the weather reminded me once more to let go of attachment. I was so full of resistance that I decided to turn my decision about the vision quest commitment over to Great Spirit. "Give me a sign," I implored. The message came quickly, loud and clear. "IF A SINGLE EAGLE SHOWS ITSELF TO YOU AGAIN BEFORE YOU LEAVE THIS PLACE, THEN THE ANSWER IS TO MAKE THE COMMITMENT."

I walked back to the fire pit that late afternoon thinking, God, I hope I don't see another eagle! It was difficult to make such a huge, long term commitment. The weather had returned to calmness, and I felt my body and spirit willing to join it regardless of the outcome.

We all gathered around the fire pit before going into the sweat lodge for our final sweat. Raven reminded us that on completion of the lodge we would gather at the fire, and those making the four year commitment would do so through the sacred pipe. The end of the quest was nearing, and I thought I was home free.

We started back to enter the sweat lodge, each woman bending low and acknowledging the ceremony upon entering. As I awaited my turn to enter the lodge, something prompted me to glance up at the mountain to the North as if a spirit helper gently nudged my focus in that direction. My eyes grew wide and my mouth parted! The moment seemed to freeze as my gaze was fixed, my body motionless. Everything around me became a blur in white mist. In what seemed like slow motion, a single eagle flew out from behind the mountain top, wings spread wide in a graceful glide, circled the top of the mountain and mysteriously disappeared. My heart leaped!

As my journey through fear continues, I know that I have the ability to ride the waves of life. Like the waves, life's challenges are continuous. There are times when I will be on the crest of the wave, times I will be in its trough and times I will be flowing and dissolving. There will also be times when I will climb onto the wing of the eagle, experience the moment and see it from a higher perspective with the broad vision of the sacred winged one.

The time had come to relinquish the Shield of Letting Go to the fire and start constructing my Shield of Power.

Exercise: *Communicate With The Gifts Of The Earth*

Find a place in nature to sit. You can take a hike to a secluded place or use your back yard. Focus on the question or concern you have and listen for the answer. It will come as a thought in your mind, clear and uncluttered by your judgments and evaluations. Hand your concern over to Great Spirit, and then listen for the answer. Listen to the messages from the animals and insects. Listen to the tallest tree or the smallest blade of grass. Accept the praise of the sun and the kisses of the wind. You are a child of the universe, of the sun and the moon, of the earth and the stars. You deserve to be here and have all that you need.

CHAPTER TWELVE

The Shield of Power

It is something that we carry within us,
and it is reflected in the way we live our lives.

I thought that in making my Shield of Power I would need to collect more from the earth to adorn it. I sit here looking at the shield, only a plain hoop made from a willow branch and realize that it is okay the way it is. As a matter of fact, it does not need to exist at all. For you see, the Shield of Power is not something tangible we need to look at and reflect upon as with the Shield of Letting Go. Instead, it is something that we carry within us, and it is reflected in the way we live our lives. So the Shield of Power is only a manifestation of the Shield of Letting Go in action. I think the significance is in the action.

How does action relate to our life purpose, our goals to meet that purpose, our higher Self in support of our purpose? Each of us has a different life purpose. Some of us know precisely what it is; others may be still wondering and searching. If you are not clear, an inner search is first advised. This can be facilitated through the use of the exercises and visualizations in this book. Consulting a professional therapist is also advised if there are issues that you need help in overcoming.

Ultimately our life's purpose is to be of service and in so doing contribute to the higher consciousness of man not only on the planet but in all of space as we know it. Our energetic source is love. When we give love out, we help to transform all of space. There are both positive and negative influences in space, and as we individually and collectively move toward filling it with love, the negative will be diminished and eventually extinguished. It takes a lot of people doing it. If you think you are ready to join this team of love givers, now is the time.

Finding out how you, as an individual, can realize your life's purpose does not have to be strain and strife. It can be exciting and enjoyable. In order to do this, we must drop the notion that we personally will gain from our effort. Of course we will. That is not the issue, but by focusing on self gain we deter the action. You may have heard that what we put out comes back to us. It is just that simple. In playing out our life's purpose we may gain respect, admiration, wealth and even celebrity status. These things are only a result of our work and rightly deserved, but do not make the mistake of playing out the wrong purpose. Self gain and greed will only add to the negative energy and not to the positive. Our focus of service needs to be outside of ourselves, and we can obtain self-fulfillment through our activity regardless of its nature if it is what fills our heart center with joy. It is this joy that we can share with the world. If you cannot *feel* it, you cannot *share* it. Maybe it is time to do what brings excitement and joy in your life. If you are depressed and discouraged about where you are in your life you are only contributing to the negative energy.

You are an energetic being—do not forget that. If you could see the energetic play between people you would probably be amazed. We can almost knock someone over with our anger and literally make them ill. Our chronic depression can also bring those around us down. The more sensitive you are the more affected you are by other people's energy. I have often heard massage therapists and

psychotherapists say they are like a sponge in pick-
ing up their client's energy (both negative and positive), and they use visualization to guard their
boundaries so they do not get overloaded. You can
imagine if you are living with a very angry or
depressed person how their energy might affect
your own. We are powerful in that we affect everyone and everything around us. That is a huge
responsibility! What do you want to do with it? I
beseech you to join the love givers by spreading
your love and joy instead of your dark mood of
hopelessness. Only you can make the choice.

As a love seeker in the past, perhaps you were
looking outside of yourself for love and acceptance. Now you can find it inside and give it out to
the world. It will come back to you. Energy flows
that way—just as we take in a breath and let it out,
the cycle will continue when your consciousness is
set to that ideal. But first things first. Assess your
life. What do you want? A healthy relationship, a
college degree, your own business? Look to see if
the relationship you are in can be transformed. If
not and you are unhappy, move on. If so, work
with your partner to make the relationship one
where you both co-create a life of individual

power. This will make the partnership powerful as well.

If you feel that you need something tangible to work with in the beginning, try making a shield and collecting power objects and building your shield (See Chapter 9) as you move toward your power—doing what you want in your life and spreading that love to others.

Your Shield of Power reflects what is in your life right now. Decide what you want to change—a relationship, job, where you live, etc. As you make these choices in your life and move ahead to what makes your energy vibrant and transcendent, add, delete or move the objects on your shield. You can see the transformation take place before your eyes. You can see that you are making progress.

There is nothing you cannot do. Go after whatever aspiration your heartfelt sense of Self aspires to. Make your life happy and fulfilling and also allow your gifts to be given to the world. The earth is your stage, and you are the lead in the play. The earth is your classroom, and you are both the student and the teacher.

Take some time to go into the wilderness and sit. Quiet the mind and tune into your heart center. *Feel* your life. Go home and write down what you want to keep, what can be transformed and what needs to be discarded. Write a list of what you want that you have not obtained because of circumstance, feelings of hopelessness and lack of control. Do these things support you living from your higher Self? Are they changes that will help you to be content and in your power and give you more as a human being to make a contribution to others and to the world? Then go for it!

Visualization: *Accessing Your Higher Self*

Find a comfortable place to sit or lie down, making sure your clothes are loose and comfortable. Take a few deep breaths and allow your body to settle down. Notice your body. What places seem to be tight and tense? Give those places permission to relax as you consciously will it. Now, using self-hypnosis, count backwards from ninety-nine to one very slowly, interjecting between each number the phrase "I am relaxed." Continue doing this until you feel relaxed and all of the muscles in your body feel loose and fluid. I use this technique when I cannot get to sleep at night, and I am usually out like a light by the time I get to seventy. So you do not want to go to sleep but instead, be comfortably relaxed. You may achieve this state by the time you reach the count of ninety or much later. Either way is okay. Have patience with yourself.

Now that you are relaxed, imagine that you are on a pathway leading into a beautiful forest. You can look down and see your feet on the path. You can look to the sides of the path and see trees, grasses, flowers, and you can look overhead and see a clear blue sky. As you are walking on the path know that there is nothing to fear—you are safe. You can see a figure walking toward you on the path. As it gets closer to you it becomes more clear. Now this figure is in front of you.

Take in all the features and characteristics of this figure so that it is vivid in your mind. Instead of "seeing" a figure you may feel or sense a presence or a light body. Notice the quality of energy surrounding the figure or presence. Does it feel light or heavy? Do you get a good, safe and loving feeling? If it feels right at this time ask the figure or presence if it represents your higher Self. You will hear or feel the answer. If it indicates "yes," ask for your purpose in this life. You may receive a lot from this first session or you may gain more insight later as you are going about your everyday activities or in the dream time at night. If you get a "no," you may ask this figure why it is on your path or you may try again at another time. Do not be discouraged. At some time you will receive the answer you are seeking.

Be clear about your intention as you go within. When you get your answer, sit with it for awhile after you come out of trance. It may be what you have already sensed but have not acted on because of fear or doubt, or it may take you completely by surprise. In either case, you do not need to do anything with it at first. Look at it, see how it can be played out in your life and if it is a path that will make a contribution to your own well being and that of others. Remember, it is never too late to make changes in your life. Consider the people around you for they may be surprised and even upset by your desire to change. Ask them for their support and love.

Once you feel confident of your purpose, start putting it in action. Write down your goals and how you can achieve them. Movement may be slow or may accelerate at a fast pace. Know that you need to act in order to make things happen. It will not get done by sitting and daydreaming or waiting for someone else to do it for you. As you move with this flow of new energy in your life check in with your higher Self using visualization. As your awareness and sensitivity to your energetic Self increases you will receive more intuitive insights and messages without effort.

There may be times when you will receive psychic flashes where a message will come when you do not expect it. The message will be very clear and you will have a feeling of surety. There will be no reason to dispute the message as you will *feel* its truth. I find that I usually get these psychic flashes when I am alone in nature, taking a leisurely walk away from the sounds and agitated energy of the city.

From this moment forward, know that you can create anything you want in your life. By practicing meditation regularly you will find it easier to be aware and in tune with your energetic being and how it flows in your life. You will find that you will become more mindful in your day to day activities, that your sense of awareness and decision making will be clearer.

You begin to wear your invisible Shield of Power. It is light, free and keeps you in touch with your higher Self. It is not permeable to outside negativism and hate. It glows and reflects love for yourself and your world.

CHAPTER THIRTEEN

Ride on the Wing of the Eagle

Riding on the wing of the eagle
is viewing life from a higher perspective.
It is swimming in the ocean of spaciousness.
It is seeing with open eyes, awareness, and love.

To be free is to fly with the eagle. Be yourself totally. Express your emotions, your feelings, your desires. Dance in the streets, run in the rain, and sing from the rooftops. Let the world know who you are. It is time to come out of hiding. Risks? Yes, there may be some. Rewards? Yes, there will be many. Fear? Sometimes, but you will ride through whatever is making you fearful in the moment.

I have come from hiding and have climbed onto the eagle's wing, and you can too. I was afraid of people, of situations, of being seen, of dying. Now, I am able to get up in front of a group and be myself without my knees shaking. I can leave a relationship that I know is not good for me. I can consciously let go of each moment. I can accept death of the body as a transformation into new life.

The eagle tipped his wing gliding toward the South, and I have to hold on a little tighter, but the ride is exciting. I can see far below where the mountains rise toward the sky and the valleys rest in their green lushness. Miles of long straight and twisting roads lie on the earth, and I can see little cars and buildings. The shoreline lies ahead. Oops! We are descending, flying low now over a huge body of ocean. The water is deep shades of blue and its surface exposes a softer shade of blue that reflects the sky, and there are little rises of white caps dancing on the top. As we get closer I can smell the salty air.

Not being able to resist another second, I stand and dive from the eagle's wing into the inviting swells of the mysterious sea feeling its cool waters envelope my body. As I swim towards the sandy bottom, I meet angel fish, blue fish, swordfish and am awestruck by the coral, plants and other strange and colorful inhabitants of this underworld fantasy. I swim to the surface and once again climb on to the wing of the eagle, and we fly to the shore.

I step down from the eagle's wing, my feet sinking into the soft, warm sand. A sea gull flies by.

I walk from the sand into a world of vegetation feeling joyful as I spy an exotic flower, a lacy fern, the heavy bark on many trees, their limbs and leaves umbrellas over the moist lush earth contrasted with the desert regions. The birds, insects and animals make themselves known—feathers, feelers, claws, fur—every color of a whirling rainbow surrounding me. With delight, I bend over and scoop up a handful of dirt and let it slip through my fingers and fall back to the earth, and I know it is what sustains me. I reach up and pluck the stars from the sky and sprinkle their light over the world, and all is illuminated.

I see the people and join them. I see those who are suffering and know that it is my suffering also. I see those who are joyful and know that it is my joy. Our colors blend, our eyes only windows into our souls. We become a chain of energy, hands joined, love linking us as we circle Mother Earth. We are each unique and separate but joined together in spirit. There is no fear in unity. We are all related.

APPENDIX

To prepare yourself for the visualizations make sure you are in a quiet comfortable place with the telephone turned off. Lie down and feel your body being supported by the surface on which you are lying. Take a few deep breaths and relax your body even more. Start with your face and proceed down your body making sure that every muscle is relaxed. Check yourself and if you still feel tightness any where, give that place in your body permission to relax. Imagine that there is a soft white light surrounding your body keeping you safe and grounded. Take another deep breath and imagine that you are inhaling this white light, letting it fill your body from the top of your head to the bottoms of your feet. Feel, sense your body become lighter as though it is slowly rising off the place where you are lying. Feel, sense your body relax even more as you are surrounded by white light and filled with white light. Slowly count down from ten to one giving yourself the suggestion to relax even more using words like relax, serene, fluid, etc.

Now that you are in a light trance state, you are ready to proceed with the visualizations described at the end of chapters one, three, nine and twelve. You will find that when you are relaxed, it will be easy for you to hear that small voice inside that connects you with your high Self. You will know it because it will be unlike the voices you hear when involved in your day to day activities. There will be more clarity and surety in the messages you receive that perhaps you do not always encounter when not in a trance state. There will be times, however, when your conscious mind will seep in and challenge the messages you get. The more you work under trance the more clarity you will encounter. At some point, you may be able to bypass the initial relaxation techniques and simply close your eyes.

Afterword

The stories and personal experiences in this book reflect my unique journey during a very special time in my life. Some of the rituals that I have shared with you, however, may not be typical of all Native American traditions. I wish to honor my own connection to the earth and spirits, and at the same time, acknowledge with great respect the traditional way of the Native American culture.

About the Author

Sheila Griffin lives in Santa Fe, New Mexico where she is a licensed therapist/hypnotherapist and a writer. She has a masters degree in Transpersonal Psychology from the Naropa Institute in Boulder, Colorado and spends much of her time traveling and facilitating workshops. Sheila has worked in the mental health field for fifteen years contributing to the journey of adolescents and adults. For more information you can contact Sheila at: sggriffin@earthlink.net.

For additional copies of this book or information on forthcoming titles go to our Web site:

http://home.earthlink.net/~sggriffin/